"Excellent...I use this book both professionally and personally. *Paren[...]* the pressure off parents and holds children accountable. I highly rec[...]
— **LIBBY CAMPBELL,** *Ph.D., therapist*

"*Parenting Without Pressure* frees parents from being nagging watchdogs and allows them to relate to their children with love, respect, healthy detachment, and positive regard."
— **EMMY K. FREEDMAN,** *Ph.D., clinical psychologist*

"I routinely ask parents whose teens come through the court system to use the *Parenting Without Pressure* approach. In over five years, I have never had a negative response from anybody I give it my highest recommendation." — **WALTER KOMANSKI,** *circuit judge*

"As a family therapist, I have relied heavily on *Parenting Without Pressure.* It provides my parents the three crucial elements for effective parenting: education on adolescent development, group support from other parents, and hands-on experience with the workbook
— **DANIELLE L. COLLETTE,** *family therapist, Permanency Program*

"When I think of parenting, I think of Teresa Langston. *Parenting Without Pressure* is a must for everyone with children. It helps make parenting enjoyable and builds stronger families."
— **JOHN A. CORCITTO,** *Ed.D., counselor, Maitland Middle School*

Parenting Without Pressure offers readers a firsthand look at ways to cope with a troubled child. Teresa's own experiences have provided support and guidance to all who have taken the time to listen
— **TERESA MILES,** *director, Boy's Town*

"Parents gain a clear, concise, easy-to-implement plan of action. Family members learn the blessings of being mutually dependent as they identify and combine their goals, values, and achievements."
— **CHARLENE MESSENGER,** *Ph.D., school psychologist, mental health therapist*

"Parents learn ways to reach the sometimes elusive goal of teaching responsibility, problem-solving skills, and developing considerate behavior in adolescents."
— **BETH SHARPE,** *Ed.D., principal, Wekiva Elementary*

"*Parenting Without Pressure* is the most commonsense approach to parenting I have seen This book gives parents a hands-on manual on how to recognize the power they have and to use it without abusing it." — **MARLENE HENDRIX,** *Juvenile Assessment Center*

"Finally a respectful approach to discipline that allows both the parent's and child's voice to be heard!"
— **PAMELA PINDER,** *caseworker, Permanency Program*

To my wonderful daughter Heather,

who chose to use her will of iron and tenacious personality

to make a positive difference in the world.

Parenting

without Pressure

A WHOLE
FAMILY
APPROACH

A PARENT'S
GUIDE

- • Directing the ADD/ADHD Child

- • Minimizing Chaos • Establishing Open Communication

- • Setting Clear Boundaries • Teaching Responsibilities

- • Managing Conflicts • Blending Families

- • Demonstrating Unconditional Love

TERESA A. LANGSTON

 PIÑON PRESS

P.O. Box 35007, Colorado Springs, CO 80935

Copyright © 2001 by Teresa A. Langston
All rights reserved. No part of this publication may be reproduced in any form without written permission from Piñon Press, P. O. Box 35007, Colorado Springs, CO 80935.

Library of Congress Catalog Card Number: 00-067656
ISBN 1-57683-214-7

Cover photo by FPG International
Cover design by Dan Jamison
Creative team: Brad Lewis, Amy Spencer, Glynese Northam

Some of the anecdotal illustrations in this book are true to life and are included with the permission of the persons involved. All other illustrations are composites of real situations, and any resemblance to people living or dead is coincidental.

This publication is designed to provide accurate and authoritative information in regard to the subject matter covered. It is sold with the understanding that the author and the publisher are not engaged in rendering legal, accounting, or other professional service. If legal advice or other expert assistance is required, the services of a competent professional person should be sought. From a Declaration of Principles jointly adopted by a Committee of the American Bar Association and a Committee of Publishers.

We have made every effort to trace the ownership of all copyrighted material and to appropriately acknowledge such ownership. In the event of any question arising as to the use of any material, we will be pleased to make the necessary changes in future printings.

Langston, Teresa A.
    Parenting without pressure / Teresa A. Langston.
        p. cm.
    Includes bibliographical references and index.
    ISBN 1-57683-214-7
    1. Parenting. 2. Parent and child. I. Title.

HQ755.8 .L3518 2001
649'.1--dc21   00-067656

FOR A FREE CATALOG OF
NAVPRESS BOOKS & BIBLE STUDIES,
CALL 1-800-366-7788 (USA)
OR 1-416-499-4615 (CANADA)

Printed in the United States of America

1 2 3 4 5 6 7 8 9 10 / 03 02 01

CONTENTS

FOREWORD

It was with delight that I reviewed Teresa Langston's *Parenting Without Pressure*. The vision, knowledge, and innovations that she provides in this how-to book are outstanding. As one of Mrs. Langston's former professors, I am justifiably proud of the tool she has created for parents to restore and maintain positive family relationships.

In this rapidly changing world, it is so easy for young people to edge into serious problems. Often they become caught in a tangle of problems that seems insurmountable to them and their parents. What is so wonderful about *Parenting Without Pressure* is that sensible, practical strategies to reestablish order and tranquility in the home are spelled out clearly. Desperate parents immediately see a glimmer of hope, a way out of the despair they have long experienced.

Teresa Langston's workbook has provided many parents with sound guidance and needed structure for restoring seriously eroded relationships, enabling parents and offspring once again to enjoy family life. However, I believe *Parenting Without Pressure* makes an even more valuable contribution to families by avoiding serious problems before they begin.

As you study and apply the strategies and principles presented here, you will almost immediately sense a renewal of love and respect among family members that might have been eroded by the everyday hassles that get in the way of caring relationships.

—WILLIAM R. BROWN, PH.D.
PROFESSOR OF SOCIOLOGY

"By wisdom a house is built,
and by understanding
it is established;
and by knowledge
the rooms are filled
with all precious and pleasant riches."
Proverbs 24:3-4
(New American Standard Bible)

ACKNOWLEDGMENTS

Writing *Parenting Without Pressure* has truly been a labor of love. However, I would never have been able to accomplish it without the assistance of some pretty wonderful folks.

I would like to extend a special thanks to Dr. William Brown, who encouraged me to put the Parenting Without Pressure concept in manuscript form. Bill has been a continual source of inspiration, and if it weren't for him, this book would not exist.

A special thanks to Trish Harris, who is responsible for introducing me to the folks at Piñon Press. Additionally, I would like to extend my appreciation to Karen Calhoun. Her years of friendship, along with her secretarial and administrative support, truly have been a blessing.

Also, I would like to thank my family, especially my daughter Renee, who provided me with much insight during the ten years we implemented the PWOP program with her.

Finally, I would like to extend my love and gratitude to my mentor, best friend, and husband, Herb. I will forever be grateful for his ability to put a positive spin on the most difficult of situations, and for teaching me the true meaning of unconditional love.

Introduction

■ ■ ■

HELP FOR PRESSURED KIDS

Guiding them around today's temptations

Today's world is very different from the world children knew a generation ago. It's a difficult time to be a young person. Kids today are on the frontline of a fast-changing world where clear definitions of right and wrong are no longer in place. Words such as *crack* and *AIDS* and *gang-banging* have been added to vocabularies as kids are forced to make decisions unknown to the same age group a generation ago: Do I want to drink or take drugs? Have sex? Join a gang? Bring a gun to school? Stay in school? Unfortunately, it's easy for even the best of kids to find themselves overwhelmed as they struggle to make good choices.

Yes, it's a difficult time for kids. But it's also a difficult time for parents. It's tough guiding children around these obstacles. Families often find themselves adrift without focus or direction because yesterday's parenting techniques no longer work. It's hard to find effective solutions, and we worry about discovering them too late.

If you're struggling with a difficult child, there's hope for you. *Parenting Without Pressure* (PWOP) can help you establish a structure that restores normal family living and prepares kids to meet today's challenges. This book offers practical parenting techniques that focus on discipline, communication, self-esteem, and unconditional love. In turn, these techniques teach children accountability, responsibility, and consequences for behavior.

However, this book isn't just for parents with challenging children. *Parenting Without Pressure* can work for anyone who wants to practice proactive parenting skills. In particular, the family workbook presents a way to be firm, fair, and consistent with discipline. It has also helped parents eliminate family fighting, enhance their children's self-esteem, and create a more positive home life.

Developed as my family struggled with an out-of-control child, *Parenting Without Pressure* provided us with a win/win format to modify our daughter's negative behavior. It also enabled us to shift our focus, thus allowing us to reinforce the good behavior we wanted Heather to repeat, to express our unconditional love for her, and to underscore her immeasurable worth as a person. With these principles we were finally able to recapture the positive aspects of our family life.

And that's the reward of *Parenting Without Pressure*. It takes the hassle out of parenting so your home can be the haven it's meant to be.

Chapter One

■ ■ ■

HOME SWEET BATTLEGROUND

Bringing structure to a faltering family

I'd always thought of us as a typical family. If we weren't like Ozzie and Harriet, we were at least like the Brady Bunch.

When I married my husband, Herb, we blended nicely into a middle-class family. As a widow, I brought eighteen-month-old Heather to our marriage and Herb, a divorced father, added his three children on the weekends. Later, a beautiful baby daughter joined us and we all adored her. As our children grew over the years, we experienced ups and downs and everyday hassles, but nothing we thought was extreme. Because Herb and I were happy and content, we thought our kids felt that way, too.

Unfortunately, by the time Heather was fourteen, she was anything but content. She was miserable, and I'm embarrassed to admit we missed it. Heather created her share of crises, but we chalked them up to adolescence. Ironically, for a while I'd been receiving "problem" phone calls from school about Heather. If someone called and asked me if I was Mrs. Langston, I wanted to ask, "Who wants to know?" If the call concerned Heather, I didn't want to be Mrs. Langston!

But we weren't seriously alarmed, and we referred to these incidents as our strong-willed daughter's "problem of the day." For too long, we assumed Heather's daily problems constituted a passing phase or peer pressure, but certainly nothing serious.

Looking back, I realize that warning signs clearly indicated Heather was in trouble. She stayed in a constant state of rebellion and refused to have anything to do with the family. She acquired a new set of friends and drastically changed her appearance. She also had problems with her teachers at school, and her grades took a nosedive. But unfortunately, we refused to see the red flags, and her problems grew worse.

It wasn't until one of Heather's high school teachers confronted us that we recognized our daughter's behavior was serious and troubled. The teacher told us Heather was failing the ninth grade, sexually acting out, and experimenting with alcohol and drugs. Finally, somebody had yanked us out of denial and into the frightening truth. It was as if we'd allowed Heather to dive into a pool without teaching her how to swim. Worse yet, we'd stood by passively and watched her almost drown.

Heather's behavior continued to deteriorate and rapidly spiraled out of control. With each act of rebellion, I reacted by becoming more authoritarian in my discipline. As I tightly held the reins and struggled for control, Heather grew more angry and defiant.

The emotional atmosphere in our family disintegrated rapidly, and soon our home resembled a battleground rather than the safe, secure, and nurturing place where our children could grow and mature. Almost everything that was being said and done was ugly, negative, and destructive. There were daily screaming matches, slammed doors, and hurt feelings—and anger and resentment grew like an ugly disease. Every day I promised myself that "today" was going to be different. I even practiced things to say to Heather when she got home from school so we wouldn't fight. But as always, something triggered the horrifying pattern and we hopelessly argued.

Everybody was miserable. And Heather, with her belligerent spirit, I-don't-care attitude, and four-letter-word vocabulary, was the most miserable of all. Years later she shared how difficult those days really were for her. She said, "Mom, every time I got off the school bus after school, I would feel sick to my stomach and wanted to throw up." I knew exactly how she felt, because when she came home, I wanted to throw up, too. What a horrible mess we were in!

DESPERATELY SEEKING STRUCTURE

If we couldn't help Heather or ourselves, we thought maybe someone else could. Fortunately, we had enough wits left to find an excellent therapist. Individually and as a family, we were in counseling for about a year. During this time, Herb and I learned many new parenting concepts and techniques.

But long after Herb and I understood the principles of good parenting, we were still left with the dilemma of *how* to put them into practice! For example, we desperately needed to shore up the structure in our home and to be consistent in disciplining our children. We needed to pull our family together, provide Heather with safe boundaries, and establish open lines of communication. Still looking for answers, we read countless articles, journals, and books—and tried what felt like almost everything. But for months we still practiced hit-and-miss parenting, with more "miss" than "hit."

The turning point came when Herb and I realized we'd never developed a plan of action or strategy for raising our children. Nor had we ever defined our goals and objectives in terms of our family. Oh, we often had talked about our hopes and dreams for our individual children. But we'd never discussed seriously how we could help them develop into mature, responsible adults.

Both my husband and I are professional people. After dinner we sometimes talk for hours about our projects, carefully outlining our plans of action. We spend time in planning because we know success doesn't just happen. It results from careful forethought and deliberate action. However, never once did we take that kind of logic and apply it to our family—until the circumstances became desperate. For the first time, we took a hard look at the reality of our family situation and began to establish realistic, workable goals, not only for our children, but also for ourselves.

As parents, we decided our overall goal was simply to "de-parent" our children; that is, move them from being self-centered, dependent (and/or out-of-control) young people to being self-reliant, independent adults. And to accomplish this, we needed to teach them everything necessary to function well as adults: the important correlation between their behavior and its consequences (both good and bad), the concepts of accountability and responsibility, and appropriate ways to solve problems and make good choices.

BASIC PARENTING PRINCIPLES

Upon reviewing these goals, Herb and I realized that many of our parenting principles were based on common-sense concepts that we'd learned by simple observation. We literally had grown up with them as they had been passed from one generation to the next. Others, however, were based on things learned more recently as we searched for methods of coping with Heather's challenging behavior.

Principles for Parenting

1. Children of all ages thrive with structure and boundaries. They need to know the rules and consequences of breaking those rules.

2. They also need the security of consistent, fair discipline.

3. Parents should always strive to separate children from their behavior. In other words, kids should clearly understand that although their behavior might be inappropriate or undesirable, they never are!

4. Healthy families are built through good communication, which is more than hearing and understanding. Good communication involves creating a safe atmosphere that allows family members to express their thoughts and feelings.

5. Kids need positive affirmation and unconditional love to build their self-esteem. Children learn more by what their parents do than by what they say. Therefore, parents should always strive to be great role models for good behavior.

Herb and I also discussed character traits or values we would like our children to acquire along the way. We based our list of character traits below on the advice of Beth Winship, syndicated columnist for the *Los Angeles Times*, who writes a column called "Growing Pains."[1]

Traits Teens Should Learn on Their Way to Maturity

1. *Responsibility.* Realizing your actions always have consequences and making yourself accountable for what they are.

2. *Self-control.* Stopping to think what is a useful and suitable reaction in a given situation instead of just "popping off."

3. *Looking ahead.* Planning your life not just around today's pleasures, but also in terms of next week, next month, next year.

4. ***Understanding.*** Learning what others think and feel, and having concern for their welfare.

5. ***Motivation.*** Developing goals in your life, as well as the desire to work hard for them.

6. ***Decision-making.*** Learning to judge a situation and make an intelligent and ap-propriate choice by evaluating the pluses and minuses, including your own values.

7. ***Love.*** Learning to give as well as receive love, and to share closeness and true concern, tenderness, and loyalty.

8. ***Self-reliance.*** When you've developed the other traits, you'll have enough faith in your own judgment and ability to run your life well, without dependence on your parents or other adults.

9. ***Confidence in oneself as an individual.*** Mature people value their own selves well enough to believe strongly in their values and goals. They care what other people think, but not to the point where they can be pressured into behavior they don't truly approve of for themselves.

CREATING THE WORKBOOK

Once Herb and I had determined exactly what we wanted to teach Heather, we developed a systematic way to accomplish it. As Heather's parents, we set about the task of writing what has become the *Parenting Without Pressure* workbook.

This workbook enabled us to parent with consistency, to tackle behavioral problems appropriately, and to develop meaningful character traits in our children. In addition, it pro-vided us with a tangible, constructive tool that was objective, fair, and nonmanipulative. And because the workbook enabled us to write down those things Heather perceived as negative (such as rules and consequences), what we said to her could be positive and uplift-ing. It literally allowed us to parent without pressure.

Putting together the first workbook was truly our labor of love for Heather. Piece by piece, we added sections to the workbook as we worked on her behavior. And when we saw the first positive changes in Heather, we began using the workbook as a preventive measure with our younger daughter.

As the months passed and Heather's behavior continued to improve, I received phone calls from parents desperate for help with their children. First, the parents of Heather's friends called, and then strangers asked for help. They, too, found that the workbook's structure helped them consistently modify their kids' inappropriate behavior and that it reinforced desirable actions. Gradually their homes were turning into positive places to live.

As word of the workbook's success spread through central Florida, local churches and schools sponsored workshops and seminars. Today, throughout the United States, psychi-atric hospitals, juvenile courts, and other agencies and organizations use the workbook with families. And families as far away as Australia and Malta utilize the workbook strategy.

But first let me say, if you're a frustrated parent, don't give up. People who attend my *Parenting Without Pressure* seminars often ask, "How is Heather doing today?" She's doing extremely well, and we are very proud of her. Heather is a licensed mental health therapist who works with troubled adolescents. Oh, Heather is still very strong willed, but now that strong will is tempered with patience and maturity. Best of all, Heather is more than a daughter to me—she's become a wonderful friend.

Herb and I can't take credit for Heather's success; she made it possible. Herb and I merely implemented simple steps that created safe parameters for Heather as she walked through some very difficult times. These steps helped us to build a bridge across the chasm of a very troubled adolescence and to make it to the other side as friends.

Chapter Two

■ ■ ■

YOUR KIDS AND THE REAL WORLD

Teaching responsibility with a family workbook

—————————————————

We all live by rules. If you don't believe it, drive down the interstate at eighty-five miles per hour, don't pay your taxes, and leave the dog in the house past potty time. Chances are very good that you're going to pay the consequences for all of the above.

Children need to learn this concept early. Unfortunately for many, they don't learn this cause-and-effect concept until later in life—and often the hard way.

In a central Florida study about juvenile delinquency and its correlation to substance abuse, it was found that many youths were surprised by their incarceration in a detention facility. Even though their individual rates of recidivism (repeated offenses) were high (an average of three times per juvenile), they attributed their return to a detention facility to a variety of external factors. Rarely did they attribute it to anything they had done.[1]

But overlooking personal responsibilities isn't a problem just for delinquent kids. As they grow toward maturity, all children need guidance in taking responsibility for their lives. And it's a parent's job to equip kids with the skills they need to move successfully from dependent children to independent adults. To do that, children should be given the privilege of doing things for themselves as early as possible. By taking increasing responsibility for picking up their toys, doing their laundry, managing their money, and getting to school on time, kids develop the necessary skills and self-confidence to manage their real world.

The *Parenting Without Pressure* workbook is divided into five sections designed to teach your children this increasing responsibility and to link their behavior to choices and consequences. As you review the workbook contents outlined in this chapter, keep in mind that if you decide to use workbooks for your children, you'll need to develop one for each child in your home. This will allow you to target each child's needs and accommodate the differences among siblings. Some parents, however, create a modified workbook system by using responsibility charts (kept on the refrigerator) instead of using the "Daily Stuff" section in the workbook, and they maintain the "Rules We Can Live By" and "Friends and Family" sections on the computer. The workbook is simply a tool; don't hesitate to modify it to work best for your family.

SECTION 1: RULES WE CAN LIVE BY

Parents often expect children to internalize the norms or rules of the household without going to the trouble of writing things down. But this chancy internalization process often doesn't take place. When a child breaks a rule, parents often hear, "I didn't understand," or "I misunderstood," or "I forgot!" Heather was an equal match for the most clear-headed adult, so I was often convinced that I was either suffering memory loss or losing my mind. Because I feared both possibilities, I devised "Rules We Can Live By" (see appendix A, page 146).

This section stresses two important concepts: arbitration and rules to live by. The rules and the consequences for breaking them must be fair and relevant to the individual child. What needs to be written for one child can be left unsaid for another.

When you begin a *Parenting Without Pressure* workbook, start with no written rules. They're to be added only as a child gives evidence that they're needed. But once the rules are written down and the consequences are established, they're the bottom line.

Arbitration is a once-a-week time that families set aside to objectively, openly, and fairly discuss anything in the children's workbooks. You can conduct family arbitrations that everyone attends and/or one-on-one meetings with each child. Individual arbitrations are helpful when it is difficult to get all family members together at the same time or if sensitive and private issues need to be discussed. Whatever the circumstances, be sure that you have a regular, established arbitration time for each child in the family.

During arbitration, everything in a child's workbook is subject to discussion and/or change, and it's the only time during the week such discussions or changes are made. If you're consistent about this, almost all of the everyday hassles with your children will be eliminated. Arbitration is a time to create new rules if necessary, acknowledge good behavior, and add new privileges. The following example shows the benefits of arbitration.

Rules We Can Live By

1. Rule: _Unplug your hot rollers after you use them._

   Consequence: _You'll lose the use of them for one week._

2. Rule: _____

   Consequence: _____

3. Rule: _____

   Consequence: _____

After using her hot rollers in the morning, Heather continually left them plugged in for long periods of time, if not all day. Because I feared a total meltdown in her bathroom, her forgetfulness turned into an everyday hassle. When I began to apply this concept from the workbook, the problem was eliminated. At arbitration I carefully explained to her why I wanted the rollers unplugged: they might burn down our house. We then established a rule that the hot rollers must be unplugged after every use. And together we decided on a consequence: If Heather left them plugged in, she would lose the hot rollers for a week.

It wasn't two days until—you guessed it—Heather left her hot rollers plugged in. The matter was handled simply by writing a message in the "Daily Stuff" section of her workbook.

Date: _____ June 29 _____

Message: ___ Heather, sorry, you left your _____

___ hot rollers plugged in. Lose _____

___ them until next Tuesday. _____

There wasn't much Heather could say. We'd discussed the need for a rule, and we'd mutually decided on a consequence. She left her hot rollers plugged in, and the consequence was the result of her behavior.

Unfortunately, parents can fall into two traps at this point. They can allow themselves to get "hooked" into discussing the consequence at the time the rule is broken. This will usually result in an argument.

They can take the path of least resistance and not follow through with the consequence. This teaches children that rules and responsibilities don't matter.

So remember, to make the *Parenting Without Pressure* program work, you must be consistent every time! This might seem difficult at first. But once the kids get the idea that rules and consequences have been fairly and objectively established—and that they stand until the next arbitration—those everyday hassles will cease. Everyone will know, up front, what is expected of him or her—every time—with no room for any misunderstandings!

One final note about arbitration: Upon starting the program, some children might be very angry and defensive at arbitration. However, hang in there! Once kids learn that the workbook and arbitration are there to stay, they'll settle down and learn how to make it work for them.

When my husband and I first started having arbitrations with Heather, not only was her attitude defensive, but her four-letter-word vocabulary was put to extensive use. She soon learned, however, that arbitration occurred only weekly and was fair, reasonable, and impartial. As she became an active participant, she quickly found that arbitration could be very beneficial for her.

By the time Heather left for college, she was articulate, well organized, and polite as she opted for her rule revisions or discussed whatever happened to be on her mind. In fact, I realized recently, she could have given any second-year law student a run for his money!

SECTION 2: FRIENDS AND FAMILY

It's horrible to discover at one o'clock in the morning that Mary, your daughter's best friend, has a different last name than her parents. Or Paul, your daughter's second-best friend, has an unlisted phone number. You don't know where your daughter is . . . and you don't have the right phone numbers.

You can eliminate this dilemma by asking your kids to complete the second section of the workbook, "Friends and Family." In this section, they fill in the names and phone numbers of friends and their parents (see appendix A, page 143). Is Mary's last name different from her folks'? No problem. Her phone number is in the workbook. If Paul's phone number is unlisted, that's no problem either. It's in the workbook, too.

Friends and Family

Emergency Numbers

Police: 911   Fire: 911   Rescue Unit: 911

Family Doctor: _Dr. Clark 593-1301_

Parents and Relatives

Mom at work: _530-3523_
Dad at work: _598-1214_
Relative: _Grandmother Stine 480-3551_
Relative: _Uncle Ron 955-7767_

Parents' Friends

Name and number: _Mr. & Mrs. Baxter 598-7128_
Name and number: _Carol Bennett 366-7788_
Name and number: _____

Neighbors

Name and number: _Mark Leming 594-2281_
Name and number: _Eva Kline 548-8630_
Name and number: _____

My Friends and Their Parents

Friend's name and number: _Kirsten Williams 471-7817_
Friend's parent cell number: _Helen Williams 471-7817_
Friend's name and number: _Joel Davis 599-7891_
Friend's parent cell number: _Don Davis 599-7891_
Friend's name and number: _____
Friend's parent cell number: _____

But this section isn't just for kids to list phone numbers. There's also space to list important phone numbers such as those for work, emergency services, and adult friends and family to call in a pinch. These are especially helpful for latchkey kids who spend time home alone each day.

Finally, this section allows parents to network with one another. This is important because it allows you to exchange information, such as the specific details for a teenager's party. It also communicates your interest and concern as a parent!

SECTION 3: FUN TIMES AND EVENINGS OUT

After too many evenings of "But Mom, I *know* I told you that's where we were going," I devised the third section of the workbook, called "Fun Times and Evenings Out" (page 142).

By utilizing this section when older children leave the house to join their friends, you'll know exactly where they'll be, who they'll be with, and what time to expect them home. That's because the kids write this information in the workbook before they go. This leaves no room for misunderstandings. The facts are in the workbook.

A Good Example

Parents can demonstrate the importance of responsibility and of being a good role model. Let your kids know when you'll be out and when you'll be home. Always leave a phone number in case of an emergency.

Signing out provides safeguards for the kids, too. One evening Heather and her friends ended up spending several hours in jail. When I arrived at the police station, Heather was a pathetic sight. She was frantic and her eyes were swollen from crying. The first thing she hysterically told me was, "It's in the workbook!"

Heather was right. She'd been in the place and with the friends she listed in the workbook. Unfortunately, neither Heather nor I realized there was a nine o'clock curfew for that area. The trespassing charge stuck.

Someone once said that trust is something you earn and should never freely be given away. This workbook section also gives children the opportunity to earn trust based on their accountability and responsibility.

As a young teenager, Heather loved to skate, so often on Saturday I would drive her and her friends to the local skating rink. Although we always had a pre-arranged pick-up time, sometimes

Fun Times and Evenings Out

Date: _9/12_

Time leaving/returning: _7:00 – 12:00 p.m._

Where I'll be: _Football game and Burger King_

Friends I'll be with: _Mary & Paul_

Date: _____

Time leaving/returning: _____

Where I'll be: _____

Friends I'll be with: _____

Date: _____

Time leaving/returning: _____

Where I'll be: _____

Friends I'll be with: _____

I would arrive early. Each time that I checked and Heather was doing everything as promised, our trust relationship grew. When this happened, Heather loved it. She'd bring this incident to our next arbitration and gain additional privileges.

However, if I checked on Heather and the situation wasn't as promised, Herb and I would simply tighten the reins and pull in her operating boundaries.

Important Point!

Trust is something that is earned. It should never be given freely. Instead, it's determined by past conduct and good decision making.

SECTION 4: DAILY STUFF

More than 12.8 million American women are the head of their household.[2] Of married women with school-age children, more than 62 percent work outside the home.[3] Yet Mom is still the primary caretaker of both the children and the household. And she needs help!

Early in life, children can learn that everyone in the family needs to pull together to run the household smoothly. Dishes don't wash themselves, beds don't get made magically, and towels don't exit the dryer already folded.

In their "Daily Stuff" sections, you simply list the chores your children are expected to complete each day (see appendix A, pages 140-141). When there were eleven wet towels on Heather's bedroom floor, there was no problem. I just opened the workbook to the "Daily Stuff" section and wrote, "Heather, please wash, dry, and fold all the dirty towels. Thank you."

When you list chores for kids, be sensitive to their schedules. Children who attend school all day essentially complete eight hours of work. If they also hold part-time jobs or attend extracurricular activities, they'll be tired. Chores are important, but one or two simple tasks (emptying the dishwasher, sweeping the floor) are probably enough for one day. Save your spring cleaning for the weekend!

We had an established rule pertaining to daily stuff: "Your daily stuff must be completed by 4:30 or you lose the use of your phone, stereo, and TV for the remainder of the day and evening." This eliminated the ritual of pleading, begging, and threatening before chores were completed.

Additionally, daily stuff provides children with many opportunities to learn responsibility. Ken Hsu, a psychiatric social worker at Meriter Hospital in Madison, Wisconsin, explains:

> There are two kinds of responsibility. There's task-area responsibility which includes the jobs you do such as cleaning your room and doing your home-

---

Daily Stuff

Date: _9/8_____

Please complete:

1. _Give the dog a bath_____
2. _Empty the dishwasher_____
3. _____
4. _____

Messages: _Hope you had a great_
day at school! I will be home
@ 4:30. Please give Mrs. Smith
a call. She wants to know if you
_can babysit tonight._____
_____I love you!_____
_____Mom_____

---

work. And there is responsibility for yourself—knowing what is right and wrong. Because children think more concretely than abstractly, it's easier for them to grasp the more concrete area of task responsibility. The more proficient they become in this area, the more capable they'll become at the abstract job of being responsible for themselves.[4]

Also important, daily stuff provides kids with the can-do feeling of doing things right. For example, competency is based on prior success. So often, the only success challenging children know is successful failure. Daily stuff gives even the most challenging child an opportunity to have daily positive successes.

Finally, daily stuff gives children opportunities to enhance self-esteem. Many parents use daily planners at work to remind them of tasks to be completed. If you ask how they feel after working their way through a list of things to do, their response is always the same—"Great!" Completing daily stuff produces the same feeling for kids. They feel great about what they've accomplished.

The added bonus from this "Daily Stuff" section is that it provides a perfect place for messages. Many children arrive home hours before their parents do, and it's nice to come home to a friendly note that says, "Hello. There's a treat for you in the refrigerator" or "I love you."

Home Alone

According to the U.S. Census Bureau, more than 1.6 million kids—including a half-million eleven years old and younger—are left alone at home each day from the time school lets out until the parent returns home from work.[5]

With this section, parents can reinforce what is positive and enhance a child's self-esteem. For example, a parent might want to comment on a particular job that was done well: "You did a wonderful job cleaning the bathroom yesterday. I especially liked the floor. Thanks!" One mom left this message: "'I'm a *positive thinker.*' Say it ten times and ask me for five dollars." The woman's son called her at the office immediately and said it ten times!

A parent's best bet?

1. *Don't always give the least desirable chores to the kids.*
2. *Limit the number of chores to two or three things.*
3. *Allow for flexibility and, when possible, rotate chore assignments.*
4. *Write a brief note every day, even if there are no chore assignments. This encourages kids to read the "Daily Stuff" section on a daily basis.*
5. *If a child is having difficulty completing his daily stuff, determine the reason at arbitration. Discuss ways you can help.*
6. *Don't expect perfection. Be realistic about what a child is capable of doing.*

Parents often find it difficult to determine the age at which kids can handle certain tasks. School psychologist Charlene Messenger, Ph.D., suggests these guidelines:

Age 2
Put pajamas away.
Pick up toys.
Undress self.
Throw out wastepaper.
Wipe up spills.

Age 3
Comb hair.
Wash face and hands.
Dress self.
Clear place at table.
Tear lettuce for salad.
Help water plants.

Age 4
Set table.
Put groceries away.
Polish shoes with damp cloth.
Help do yard work.
Dust furniture.
Get mail.
Put dirty clothes in hamper.

Age 5
Pour own drink.
Clean mirrors and windows.
Fold clothes and put them away.
Clean out car.
Feed pet and clean its living area.
Make own sandwich.
Make bed.

Age 6
Choose clothing for day.
Shake rugs.

Water plants.
Peel vegetables.
Hang up clothes.
Tie own shoes.

Age 7
Prepare own school lunch.
Rake leaves and weeds.
Take pet for walk.
Care for own minor injuries.

Age 8
Run carpet sweeper.
Organize magazines and mail.
Take out trash.
Empty dishwasher.
Clean out silverware drawer.
Help prepare meals.
Fold and put away family laundry.

Ages 9 to 11
Wash countertops.
Keep bathroom tidy.
Help plan grocery lists.
Do dishes independently.
Wash car with supervision.
Help do laundry.
Take total care of pet.

Age 12 and Up
Do laundry independently.
Do yard work.
Prepare family meals independently.
Clean living area and own room.
If sufficiently mature, supervise young children.

SECTION 5: ANYTHING AND EVERYTHING GOES

This last section is a place to keep miscellaneous items such as school progress reports, family contracts, and subjects to discuss at arbitration that might otherwise be forgotten. It's the place where "anything and everything goes." For example, Jared's parents were desperate to eliminate the ongoing battles with him. PWOP's workbook system enabled them to diffuse the daily fighting. Jared's parents implemented a *disobeying rule* that took care of all willful acts of disobedience. Here they listed all other annoying or inappropriate behavior to discuss at arbitration. This helped reduce their frustration, because it allowed them to vent in an appropriate place and it eliminated their need to nag daily. More important, it provided a place to list things Jared was doing right and allowed them to layer arbitration with comments about his good behavior.

With Heather, in addition to noting arbitration discussion items and contracts, we kept track of her school progress reports.

Weekly Progress Reports

To monitor Heather's performance at school, we required that she bring home a progress report. During the two years that we tracked Heather's progress, we simply required her to earn a C, or 2.0 grade point average, for the week in each of her subjects (see appendix A, page 148). This earned her the privilege of going out with friends on weekends. Each Friday it was Heather's responsibility to take the progress report to each of her teachers. And because we requested weekly reports at parent/teacher conferences, Heather's teachers readily provided the information.

Heather's C average may not seem suitable for your children, but it was a realistic goal for her at that stage. This was the only way we got Heather through the ninth grade.

If you have to make a similar decision for one of your children, your frame of reference should be (1) where your child is starting academically, and (2) what he can realistically obtain.

Weekly Progress Report

Name: Ann

For week of: February 7-11

Class period	Subject	Teacher	Numerical grade point average
1st	Spanish	Wilson	2.8
2nd	Algebra	Webb	1.9
3rd	Science	Jamison	2.3
4th	Art	Miller	2.4
5th	English Lit	Johnson	2.1
6th			

Family Contracts

At one time, it seemed Heather was on a first-name basis with every police officer within twenty miles of our home. After she received several tickets, Herb and I decided enough was enough. We asked her to draw up a contract stating how she planned to be a more responsible driver and, of course, pay her tickets. We all agreed on the terms, signed the document (see appendix A, page 149), and placed it in the "Anything and Everything Goes" section of the workbook.

Don't hesitate to make similar contracts with your kids. Your family's contracts will model and teach responsibility.

Family Contract

Name: _Heather_

Subject: _Tickets for speeding_

Desired Behavior: _Be a responsible driver._

How it will be accomplished: _Pay to go to driving school. Also pay tickets by working at home._

Consequences and/or incentives: _You'll lose your license._

Heather Langston   _5/21_
Child's Signature: Date:

Herb Langston   _5/21_
Parent's Signature: Date:

THINGS TO DISCUSS AT ARBITRATION

Use the "Things to Discuss at Arbitration" page to list things that should be discussed at arbitration (see appendix A, page 139). Whether they're troublesome areas that need correcting or behaviors that should be praised, you can eliminate the possibility of forgetting them simply by listing them here.

For example, my younger daughter, Renee, had trouble remembering to turn off the lights in her bedroom. We decided at arbitration that for every light she left on, I'd deduct fifty cents from her allowance. In the "Anything and Everything Goes" section, I kept track of the lights left on and how much allowance I owed her—or what amount she owed me— at the end of the week!

Things to Discuss at Arbitration

1. Date: _3/13 sarcastic note_
2. Date: _3/16 dirty dishes_
3. Date: _3/17 phone bill_
4. Date: _3/20 doing well in school_
5. Date: _3/20 missing blouse_
6. Date: _3/21 not fighting with sister_
7. Date: _____
8. Date: _____

MORE THAN JUST PAPER

Unfortunately, most parent/child arguments involve mundane things such as chores, curfew, clothing, and homework. Far too often, parents get sidetracked with these minor issues, resulting in a daily communication pattern of nagging and fighting. Because the workbook and arbitration provide a constructive format for resolving conflict, parents are free to develop supportive family relationships and create positive lines of communication.

Recently, a family shared how well this worked for them. Both parents worked and didn't arrive home till 6:30 P.M. By implementing the workbook system, they literally rediscovered their family! Freed from the ongoing "When are you going to do your homework?" or "Why haven't you taken out the trash?" type of communication that had prevailed for years, they could spend time getting to know their children. Family dinners and evenings were spent laughing, talking, and sharing their lives.

Another family found that by not continually fighting over little things, the family members were less defensive and therefore more responsive to open discussion about relevant topics such as peer pressure and social issues.

ENABLING PARENTS

Help Kids Get Ready for the Real World

It's a parent's responsibility to prepare children for the real world. This preparation includes teaching them the skills needed to successfully make the transition from dependent children to independent adults. Parents accomplish this education by . . .

Giving children increasing responsibility for managing their own lives. Kids should be allowed the privilege of doing as much as they can for themselves as early as possible. By taking increased responsibility for their laundry, managing their money, getting to school or a job on time, and so on, they develop needed skills and gain self-confidence. They also learn that adult life isn't all fun and games.

Refusing to enable by making excuses. Making excuses for children such as "If I didn't get him up, he'd never get to work on time," "If I don't check his homework, he will never get it right," or "If I don't pay the fine, he will go to jail" only fosters dependency and spawns trouble. *Teenagers need to know that their lives are their responsibilities.*

Why Is It Important?

For a better understanding, consider the analogy of the Olympic-size pool:

Imagine that the real world with all of its possibilities is an Olympic-size pool filled with brilliantly clean fresh water. The diving board of that pool is the home you've made for your family. While your children are on that diving board, your responsibility as parents is to teach them how to swim. You accomplish this by teaching them all the important strokes—the breast stroke, back stroke—that is, to be accountable, to make good choices and decisions, and to face the consequences of their behavior.

Parents know that sooner or later everyone must swim in the pool. Furthermore, they know that pool can mean one of two things for children: It can be something exciting, wonderful, and fun. Or it can be deadly. It all depends on how well they can swim.

However, in addition to being able to swim well, kids need to be cautioned about the baggage they acquire while on the diving board. This baggage can be alcohol or drug abuse or addiction, unwanted pregnancies, inadequate education, or a criminal record. Although kids may be excellent swimmers, if they're loaded down with baggage, they still will have a difficult time staying afloat.

Kids should be taught early that it's their life and that one day they'll have to swim in the pool. Parents need to stress the importance of learning to swim well, free of baggage.

CHOICES AND THEIR LINK TO BEHAVIOR

Parents can't control their children's behavior. Unfortunately, too many frustrated parents try unsuccessfully. However, parents can teach children to control their own behavior. Start by teaching children that *behavior doesn't happen in a vacuum. It's the result of choices.* Focus on the mechanics of making good decisions and appropriate choices. Start early by giving children the opportunity to practice making simple decisions. For example, allow a kindergartner to choose between two outfits of clothing each morning or a teenager to choose between taking French or Spanish at school. Also, let a child accept the responsibility for his choices. For example, don't provide movie money for a teen who has spent his allowance. By learning to make decisions and appropriate choices, children develop the needed skills to think for themselves and gain confidence in their own judgment.

What If Someone Wanted You to . . .

- drink at a party?
- take drugs?
- have sex?
- skip school?
- bring a gun to school?
- smoke a cigarette?

A parent's best bet?

1. Let your children practice making choices. Giving your kids opportunities at early ages to make simple decisions is the basis for independent thinking.

2. Teach kids to stop and think. Role-play negative situations that children are likely to face by asking, "What if . . . ?" Talk about possible consequences and offer suggestions if necessary. Furthermore, use arbitration as an opportunity to evaluate problems properly and arrive at appropriate solutions. Finally, reward, reward, reward good choices.

3. Allow children to experience the consequences of their choices.

KNOWING WHERE TO START

Examining the Behavior

Dr. Rudolf Dreikurs, a highly respected child psychiatrist, categorized four basic goals of misbehavior: attention, power, revenge, and the display of inadequacy.[6] When coping with a child's inappropriate behavior, examine his motive. Does he need attention or need to control? Or is he feeling helpless or inadequate? Carefully examine and understand the purpose of the behavior. Also, if the inappropriate behavior is ongoing, seek the help of a competent mental health therapist or counselor.

Fixing the "Monster"!

Remember, you can't modify behavior if you can't identify it.

I will never forget the heartbreak expressed by a mom who recently attended a *Parenting Without Pressure* workshop. The class participants were asked to introduce themselves and briefly describe their children. Her description of her children was simply: "What can I say about my boys? They're just a couple of monsters."

One might ask, "How do you fix a monster?" You don't. But you can modify behavior, if you can identify it.

My Child's Behavior

I like	I dislike
Kind to brother	Swears
Honest with money	Smokes
Sense of humor	Sloppy
Creative	Poor grades

Many times parents are overwhelmed with children's inappropriate behavior and are at a loss to know where to start. To help determine a starting point, fold a sheet of paper lengthwise. On one side, write everything you like about the child's behavior. On the other side, write everything you dislike about his behavior. (See page 145 in appendix A.) On the dislike side, prioritize the list in order of importance. Pick the top four or five things and formulate rules and consequences for each. Write the rules and consequences in the "Rules We Can Live By" section of the child's workbook. *Then spend your time, energy, and effort reinforcing the good behavior.*

DIGGING FOR GOLD

Transforming kids into responsible people takes time and hard work. However, while they're developing their ability to make good choices, you can shift your focus to what they're doing right and the actions you want repeated.

Think for a minute about an old-time prospector. He'll probably shovel a great deal of dirt before he ever hits gold. Yet despite the huge mounds of shoveled dirt, his attention never wavers. His focus on the gold is constant. You see, he's never sidetracked by the dirt because he always remembers the incredible value of the gold.

Unfortunately, parents can shovel a lot of "dirt" when dealing with a child's negative behavior. However, if you always remember the importance of the "gold," you'll be able to maintain your focus there.

This is more easily accomplished with the *Parenting Without Pressure* workbook. It provides the everyday structure that you need to cope with inappropriate behavior while you look for your children's best. This enabled us to shift our focus and spend our time and energy on Heather's good behavior and remind her that she really was capable of accomplishing wonderful things.

MAKING YOUR PWOP WORKBOOKS

Children in families always come in an assortment of shapes, sizes, and ages, with a variety of temperaments and personalities. Parents will find that a rule that has to be written for one child can be left unsaid for another child. That is one reason workbook contents will vary from child to child. Because of this, it's necessary to make a workbook for each child, following these steps:

1. Purchase a five-tab spiral notebook, the kind often sold at grocery stores. One should last about four months.
2. On each of the tabbed pages, write the name of a workbook section: (a) Rules We Can Live By, (b) Friends and Family, (c) Fun Times and Evenings Out, (d) Daily Stuff, and (e) Anything and Everything Goes.
3. One alternate method is to use a three-ring binder and copy the workbook pages found in appendix A. Simply add workbook sheets as needed.
4. For younger children, eliminate the sections that don't apply, such as the "Friends" part of "Friends and Family." (You probably know all your children's friends because they're neighbors.)
5. Ask older kids to fill in the information about their friends in "Friends and Family." After they've used the program for a while, some families simply recopy these lists from the previous workbooks. Our children kept a list of their friends on our home computer. With each new workbook, they simply revised their list, printed it, and stapled it in the "Friends and Family" section of their new workbook.
6. When you start a new workbook, recopy only the rules pertaining to daily stuff and the general disobeying rule (see page 42). Because both are utilized often, it's best to keep these handy. However, all the other rules from past workbooks should stay in effect. Ideally, by now they have been internalized and are permanently deposited where they should have been all along—in the children's memory banks!

SUGGESTIONS ABOUT HOW TO USE *PARENTING WITHOUT PRESSURE*

These guidelines will help the workbook system run smoothly for your family:

1. Remember that the workbook is simply a tool. Modify it to work best for your family.
2. At the first family meeting, explain the program and the workbooks. Focus on the positive aspects and the benefits to everyone. Be sure to say this is a win/win strategy that tangibly emphasizes behavior and its consequences, both positive and negative. Set the time for your next meeting, allowing everyone the opportunity to prepare for it.
3. The second time your family meets, create individual *Parenting Without Pressure* workbooks or responsibility charts (found on page 26) with your children. Give the children the opportunity to discuss their concerns and problem areas. Then from your list of likes and dislikes, discuss your specific areas of concern. Establish a specific time for upcoming arbitrations.

4. As the family familiarizes itself with the workbook during the first week of implementation, use only the "Rules We Can Live By" and the "Daily Stuff" sections. This will give everyone the opportunity to begin to understand the program and prepare for the first arbitration.

5. Some parents find it necessary to start with rules concerning daily stuff and willful disobedience. When you present these for the first time, follow these examples:

   - Daily stuff rule: "Daily stuff must be completed by *(specific time)*. If that doesn't happen, *(specific consequence)."* Without this rule, you could be asking, pleading, and begging your children to complete their assigned chores.
   - Disobeying rule: "Any willful act of disobedience will result in *(consequence)."* This rule covers inappropriate behavior that currently doesn't have a rule and consequence. (The disobeying clause is discussed more fully on page 42).

The second week will be the toughest. It's not unusual for some children, especially teenagers, to attempt to sabotage the program during week two. But hang in there! Once everyone realizes it's a permanent part of family life, the kids will settle down and make it work for them.

Arbitration Day is just that: a time to arbitrate. Listen to the kids. Be as fair as you can. Try to address their needs every time. Let them help formulate their own rules and consequences. Remember, however, that you're the parent, and the final decision about anything rests with you.

Refuse any challenges to do battle outside of arbitration. Allow the rules, consequences, daily stuff, and contracts to take effect without comment during the week. And don't try to "out-fight" kids at arbitration. You can't! But you can out-think them. Simply ask yourself, "What do I want to see happen here, and how can I accomplish it?"

Be consistent and follow through every time. Children can be tough and manipulative. Once they learn to badger a parent out of consequences, a contract, or daily stuff, you've lost—and will have to regain—that ground.

Keep workbooks in a central area such as the kitchen. When the kids carry them off to other parts of the house, they'll get lost. The workbooks need to be in a location where they'll be seen often by the children (perhaps the kitchen table), because they're responsible for reading the workbooks and accomplishing their daily stuff. If you're using a responsibility chart, post it on the refrigerator door.

Each evening, fill out the "Daily Stuff" section for the next day. This eliminates additional stress in the morning when you're trying to get the family to work and school on time. Responsibility charts can be filled out on the weekend for the following week.

Remind your children often that there's no "split camp" in your home. You're all on the same team. Frequently remind them of your love. Continually look for the best in your kids, and when you find it, always show it to them.

Chapter Three

■ ■ ■

Rules We Can Live By

Establishing effective rules and boundaries

Imagine you're driving a car on a two-lane bridge over a river. What side of the road do you drive on? Now imagine you're crossing the bridge again a few days later. The night before, a storm washed out the guardrails. What side will you drive on this time? You'll probably switch from staying on the right side to hugging the middle of the road unless traffic comes from the opposite direction. Though you didn't realize it, the guardrails had provided you with a sense of security.

Structure is like that for children. In a real and practical sense, providing structure is the most "freeing" thing you can do for kids. It offers safety and gives guidance so they can grow and mature. It helps them learn about consequences and behavior. And within secure parameters, it teaches them to exercise good judgment. You can build this emotionally secure structure for your children by establishing operating boundaries and household rules for them.

SETTING BOUNDARIES

Operating boundaries are the parameters in which children can safely and reasonably conduct their lives and grow toward maturity. These boundaries include responsibilities, which are those behaviors you require from your children, and privileges, which are the acknowledgments your children receive for responsible behavior. For example, older children are responsible for returning home by a certain time at night. If they consistently stay within this boundary, they could receive the privilege of staying out an hour later on the weekends.

Boundaries Based on Age

Generally, two factors will affect your children's boundaries. The first and most obvious is age, because it's a measure of their maturity. Seven-year-olds can't possibly carry the same responsibilities as sixteen-year-olds, so their boundaries take different shapes.

Younger Kids, Older Kids

Often kids who hang out with older kids find themselves in situations for which they are not ready. Such a child is more likely to cave in to social pressure and to try risky behaviors involving drugs and sex because he or she desperately wants to be accepted by older friends.

The Basics of Boundaries

School night curfews:

■ Kids should be home by dinner, except for specific activities approved by parents.

Weekend and holiday curfews:

■ Sixth grade: 10:00 P.M.
■ Seventh and eighth grades: 10:00 to 11:00 P.M.
■ Ninth and tenth grades: 11:00 P.M. to midnight.
■ Eleventh and twelfth grades: 11:00 P.M. to 12:30 A.M.
■ Curfews should not exceed 12:30 A.M. unless there's a special occasion.
■ Be awake or have your kids wake you up when they get home.

Dating ages:

■ High school: dates should be no more than two years older than your child
■ Middle school: supervised group activities only
■ Double dating: age 15
■ Single dating: age 16

Other activities:

■ Teenage nightclubs: teens 17 or 18 years old
■ Peer parties: middle and high school students should never attend unchaperoned parties. Obtain the host parents' names, address, and phone number. Call ahead and verify the occasion and ask questions about supervision and the alcohol and drug policy.
■ Rock concerts: older teens can attend together if they're fulfilling their responsibilities. Younger teens, never without adult supervision.
■ Mall shopping: alright for older teens. Younger teens only for a short period of unsupervised time.

For many parents, age-appropriate boundaries can be difficult to discern. In the box above is a list of boundaries suggested by Dr. John Crocitto, a middle school counselor. Because younger children don't usually leave home by themselves, these boundaries apply to middle and high school students.

Younger children often want to mimic what older kids do. Somehow, the activities of older kids seem more exciting and give young children a chance to feel "grown up." But it's a parent's responsibility to exercise caution, even when kids scream, "I can handle it!" or "Everyone's doing it!" Translated, that could mean anything from attending unchaperoned parties to drinking and using drugs.

When you give children more freedom than they can handle—when you let them reach beyond their years—it's a surefire way for them to fail. To ease the pressure at home, some parents allow younger kids the same freedom given to their older counterparts, but this can place those younger children in danger. They're less mature, more inexperienced, and less capable of handling the unexpected—and certainly no match for the older kids they'll be "hanging out" with.

Age-based boundaries were a heated topic of conversation with my youngest daughter, Renee. She'd always been an easy child to parent, making good personal choices and earning top grades at school. Then at fourteen, she fell for a young man four years her senior. She wanted to date this new boyfriend, and at every point possible she reminded us that she was a good kid (which she was) and that Steve was a decent guy (which he was). So why couldn't they date?

It was a tough call. Both teens were all a mom could hope for, and Renee acted mature for her age. I genuinely wanted to please her, to allow her the freedom. But I knew I might be setting her up for a fall. Renee just wasn't old enough; she didn't have the experience to pull off dating someone eighteen years old. Although she often acted older and wiser, there were times she did behave like a fourteen-year-old, or even younger.

As her parent, those were the times I needed to remember and be prepared for. As much as I wanted to say yes, I had to say no.

Finally, I told Renee, "Imagine you're standing on a stepladder. As a freshman just starting high school, you're on the bottom rung. Right now, you're doing all of the fun things appropriate for a fourteen-year-old. However, as an eighteen-year-old senior, Steve is at the top of the ladder. He's enjoying all of the freedom, responsibilities, and privileges for a young man his age.

"If you date Steve, where will you end up on the ladder? Is Steve going to be satisfied coming back to the ladder's bottom rung with you? Or will he want to pull you up the ladder to what's appropriate for him?

"Steve will want to pull you up the ladder. Now, I know you handle yourself well, but I'm not certain how you'd manage at the top of the ladder. Even though you're responsible, you don't have the experience and maturity that only years can give."

It made her unhappy, but even though Renee couldn't date, we welcomed her friends into our home. As for Steve, he and Renee often saw one another at church and occasionally spent evenings on the porch swing under the watchful eye of her dad and me. And they have remained friends for years. By not allowing Renee to date someone much older, she was able to safely explore the boundaries of appropriate relationships with friends her own age.

Work hard on setting your kids up for success by establishing age-appropriate boundaries.

Boundaries Based on Actions

The second factor that affects children's boundaries is their conduct, particularly as reflected in their personal workbooks. Did your kids complete their chores? Did they tell you where they were going with friends? Did they obey household rules? By their actions in the past, kids determine how many and what kinds of responsibilities and privileges they'll have in the future.

All children who have slipped into serious trouble will need tight parameters initially. Key behavioral issues that require limited boundaries are drug and alcohol use, sexual promiscuity, truancy from school, running away from home, or other uncontrollable or serious delinquent behavior. These kids need a short rope and high accountability for the special rules that govern their behavior.

Conversely, operating boundaries can be expanded for children who behave well, still keeping in mind what's appropriate for their age levels. Key behavioral issues for these kids are completing their daily stuff and obeying household rules.

Because operating boundaries relate to behavior, these parameters will probably expand and contract according to your children's conduct and their move toward maturity. As I explained in the last chapter, when we required Heather to maintain a C average in each of her classes, we rewarded her with the privilege of going out with friends on weekends. After a while, when she consistently brought home the required grade or better, we gave Heather a later curfew and allowed her to ride home in a friend's car after school.

But then one of Heather's teachers called us. She said that Heather was failing algebra class and had been filling out her own progress reports! Immediately, we pulled in Heather's boundaries and she lost her weekend and after-school privileges.

When it's necessary to pull in their boundaries, it's also tempting to nag your children about their bad behavior. It's important to discuss their bad choices, but repeated harping probably won't change your kids' actions. Focus, instead, on affirming their progress toward better behavior. After the algebra incident, we focused on Heather's behavioral progress by stating how well she was doing in other areas, like completing her daily stuff. We kept reminding her that she could make good choices. And it wasn't long until, because of her good behavior, we extended Heather's boundaries again.

Knowing Where to Start

After deciding to define boundaries for your kids, it's challenging to decide where to start. These guidelines can help you, as needed, to effectively set and move boundaries.

Knowing Where to Start

- Start with those things that are important.
- Frequently check on behavior. With out-of-control children, leave nothing to chance.
- Express a positive, affirming attitude.
- Increase responsibilities along with privileges.

Start with those things that are important. Especially with troubled children, work diligently on correcting what's out of control and temporarily let everything else go. These issues will vary from household to household and from child to child. For one family, the daughter staying in school was the key issue, not whether or not she wore safety pins for earrings. One son repeatedly set fire to the grass at school. His mom decided his knuckle-cracking habit was the least of her worries. If your daughter keeps running away, her messy bedroom can take a back seat for a while.

By not trying to correct everything at once, you won't overkill the situation. And you won't risk winning a battle but losing the war, even with children with less-troubling problems.

The Monitor

"One of the functions of parents is monitoring—you monitor their homework, their friends, what they're really doing in their spare time. I don't think we've said enough to parents about how the demands on them change when early adolescence hits, and kids may start to engage in drugs and sex. Monitoring is critical."[1]

Frequently check on behavior. For out-of-control kids it's especially crucial to leave nothing to chance. Unfortunately, there's no room to short-change this step. It requires a great deal of time, energy, and effort, but you'll obtain an objective measure of their behavior and a tangible tool for arbitration. Also, you'll communicate to the kids that you care enough to stay involved with them.

At this stage, boundary restrictions might include:

- earlier curfews for evenings out
- monitoring school grades and daily attendance
- making sure children are where they said they'd be on evenings out
- screening for possible drug use

When children successfully follow through with their restrictions, they earn or reestablish your trust in them. If they comply with the items on their lists, you can loosen their boundaries. If they don't measure up, renew their restrictions on a short-term basis. Kids can handle tough restrictions for a week at a time, especially if their conduct determines how tight their restrictions will be the next week.

Express a positive, affirming attitude. When you implement boundaries, your attitude will affect how well they're received. Avoid an I'm-going-to-get-you approach. Try to be positive and encouraging. And every time you check and your kids are doing what they're supposed to do, praise them for it. Let them know that they can use their cooperative behavior as a bargaining point at arbitration. For example, in one family the son wanted to use the family car. Instead of demanding that privilege, he came to arbitration prepared with examples from his workbook of responsibility and good behavior. His parents, genuinely pleased by his progress and this logical approach, readily agreed to let him use the car.

Also, be sure to commend kids when they don't repeat their poor behavior. For example, chronic runaways leave home for a variety of reasons, but often it's to avoid conflict with their parents. When parents fight with a teen who has run away before and the child doesn't leave, the affirmation could be, "I'm proud of you. You really showed me a lot of maturity. Instead of running, you're staying and dealing with some tough issues." This type of affirmation validates good choices and reinforces positive behavior.

If children haven't been successful in turning around their behavior, implement the consequences without commenting on the failure. If it's impossible not to comment, without being sarcastic say something like "That wasn't one of your better choices." Remember to look for areas where your kids have made good choices—especially if they have poor success rates—and comment on those.

Increase responsibilities along with privileges. After your children improve their most pressing behavior problems, it's time to expand their boundaries. Still, their lives shouldn't be all privileges and no responsibilities. As you increase their boundaries, you should also expand their responsibilities. To the list of responsibilities for teens you could add eliminating obscene language, accomplishing chores, or showing courtesy to family members. For younger children, you could add completing homework on time and not provoking siblings. This way, you'll create a continuum of personal change, emotional growth, and maturity.

When Heather abandoned her alcohol and drug use—and passed the ninth grade—we expanded into other areas of responsibility. As a sophomore, she not only earned acceptable grades, but she also made her bed in the morning, did her own laundry, and cleaned up her vocabulary. During that year, a four-letter word cost her five dollars, but she rarely owed us money for any obscenities.

During the four-and-a-half years that we practiced the *Parenting Without Pressure* program with Heather, her boundaries expanded and contracted many times. But when she entered college, her boundaries were so loose, she was making almost all of her own decisions. Now that's progress!

GUIDELINES TO SAYING YES

I made many mistakes parenting my kids, and one was that I said no too many times. In fact, I restricted so many things that Heather quit listening altogether. Because I desperately wanted her to turn down dangerous activities such as alcohol and drug use, I started working on saying yes to as much as possible.

Peg Ley, a family therapist, helped me determine the requests to which I could say yes. She suggested that parents should say yes as long as the answer is no to the important questions below.

Saying No Can Mean Yes

- Is it illegal?
- Is it immoral?
- Is it inappropriate for the child's age?
- Is it going to hurt the child or anyone else?
- Is it something that will make a difference in five years?

At arbitration, a fifteen-year-old boy announced to his mother that he wanted to dye his hair blue. The mom felt horrified, but then she examined the facts. Her son was an honor-roll student who behaved responsibly. After asking herself the five questions, she decided to say yes. In fact, she dyed his hair for him. Although the son hated his dyed hair and soon cut it off, the mother gained lots of credibility with her son.

Does this mean your kids are entitled to blue hair? Not necessarily. But carefully pick your battles—and say yes to as much as possible, using the questions as a guide.

Each time you say yes, note that in the "Anything and Everything Goes" section of the workbook. Then when you say no in the future, you'll be prepared when a child yells, "You're not fair!" You can reply, "I understand how you feel, but on March 14, April 9, and June 8, I said yes. However, this time I'm saying no."

ESTABLISHING HOUSEHOLD RULES

Effective discipline requires that you make parental expectations very clear by establishing clear household rules. However, a common mistake made by many parents is to have too many household rules. They have written rules for everything. As a result, they become frustrated when none of them is followed. Because rules for rule's sake will not work, establish rules only when necessary. You need rules for three basic areas only:

1. ***To provide guidelines:*** A guideline is a rule without a consequence. It clearly defines parental expectation for children's behavior. For example: No entertaining friends of the opposite sex in your bedroom. Or, no one outside the family is allowed inside the house unless Mom and Dad are home.

2. **To define boundaries:** Again, a boundary is a rule without a consequence. It simply defines privileges, such as an 8:30 bedtime or a midnight curfew.

3. **To modify behavior:** Behavior modification is a written rule with a consequence formulated specifically to modify or change a child's behavior. This also includes boundaries and guidelines not followed by simply making a request. For example: "If you're not home and inside by midnight, on the very next date night you must be home by 11:00 P.M."

When establishing household rules for your family, remember these key points:

Let the kids help. This communicates that you want to be fair and that you care about their feelings. Also, when kids have the opportunity to participate in making the rules and consequences, they're much more likely to follow them. It's hard to argue with something they've had a part in formulating.

One parent said her son always left the radio at maximum volume after driving the car. Because she was continually being blasted out of the front seat, she brought this up for discussion at arbitration. Her son agreed to try to remember to turn down the radio after using the car and suggested he'd wash and wax it if he forgot.

Participation

To participate in something is to have ownership in it. Therefore, as much as possible, allow the kids to participate in formulating their rules and consequences. A kid will be much more willing to follow a rule that he was responsible for making!

Be specific about the rules and consequences. Never deal in generalities. A rule that says, "Please be home on time or you'll be in trouble," only leads to arguments. It's better to write, "You must be home and inside by midnight or your curfew for the next date will be 11:00 P.M."

Very quickly, kids will use the workbook to their advantage. They'll work overtime at finding loopholes. This happened to a dad who hadn't been specific about his son's curfew. When the young man walked through the door at 1:00 A.M., the father angrily announced to his son, "You're an hour past your curfew!" His son looked surprised.

"But Dad," he said, "I was home at midnight. I was outside talking to my friends!"

You can eliminate problems like this by being specific.

Unfortunately, some people must control every aspect of their children's lives, and consequently, end up with rules, rules, rules. Then they're surprised when their kids disobey. If you create too many rules or unnecessary rules, your kids probably won't comply, just to get some breathing space.

Explain the necessity of each rule. When a child asks why, it's no longer acceptable to say, "Because I said so!" Take the time to explain the rationale behind household rules. This will help children clearly understand the necessity for the specific restrictions or rules.

A single mother of a fourteen-year-old boy shared this household rule and the necessity behind it: "No swimming in the backyard pool when an adult is not home." She explained to him that this was a safety issue. In case of an emergency, a responsible adult might be needed.

When applying the rules, be consistent and fair. As I mentioned earlier, consistency is the key to a parenting program's success. But it's your fairness that will win over kids more than anything else. Fairness includes giving your children "the benefit of the doubt" as much as possible.

You can determine how much leeway to give by consulting the children's notebooks. For example, a child arrives home twenty-five minutes late and says his friend's car had a flat tire. If his workbook reflects that normally he's been coming home on time, chances are he's telling you the truth. You can let him off the hook. On the other hand, if he's had several questionable incidents in the last month or has been late frequently, there's probably reason to doubt the alibi. You'll need to enforce the consequence.

When you give your children the benefit of the doubt, be sure to note it in the "Anything and Everything Goes" section of their workbooks. If at some point someone screams that you're not fair, again, you'll have a record of the times you've been understanding.

Start with rules you can enforce. Otherwise, kids will manipulate their way out of the consequences. I dealt with this problem when Heather kept smoking despite my rule that she should not. This habit turned into a heated issue at our house. When Heather went out with friends, she often smelled like smoke when she returned home. In an outrage, I'd accuse her of smoking and, of course, she'd deny it and the argument was on!

In reality, I couldn't prove that Heather had been smoking, even though I felt certain about it. Therefore, I changed the household rule about smoking. At arbitration, I revised the rule to say, "You may not smoke in my presence or in our home. If I find cigarettes in your possession, I'll throw them out and deduct their cost from your next week's allowance." I revised the rule so Heather would learn that broken rules have consequences; she couldn't disobey and get away with it. I created a rule I could enforce.

Always include a disobeying rule. This rule takes care of willful, defiant behavior for which there is no rule. Because many times this is going to be a judgment call on the part of the parent, this is the most subjective aspect of the workbook.

A week after Heather's grandfather purchased a new Cutlass Supreme, he left town on business for two weeks. He didn't want to leave the car unattended in his driveway, so he parked it at our house for safekeeping. Imagine my reaction when Heather took the car, loaded with friends, to the beach for several hours. We didn't have a rule that said Heather couldn't take her grandfather's car to the beach. But without a doubt, she knew she'd committed an infraction. That's when I fell back on the disobeying rule.

Heather's disobeying rule said, "Any act of willful disobedience will result in Heather being grounded until the next arbitration. At that arbitration, we will discuss if an additional consequence should be added." Heather's consequence? Because we'd just had an arbitration, she was grounded for a week. At the next arbitration, we decided Heather would lose her phone and TV privileges for the next two weeks and write a letter of apology to her grandfather.

PULLING IT TOGETHER

When Herb and I established boundaries and rules for our daughters, we learned some timeless principles helpful for pulling everything together. They're taken from the best-selling book *The Strong-Willed Child*, by Dr. James Dobson.[2]

"Define the Boundaries Before They're Enforced"

"Always establish reasonable expectations and boundaries in advance. Children should know what's expected of them before they're responsible for it. If you haven't defined it, don't enforce it."

Before I understood this guideline, I'd sometimes blame Heather for breaking a rule when we'd never clearly defined the rule or its consequence. How unfair for her! When this happened—and it wasn't a case of willful, defiant behavior—I apologized. Then I noted what Heather had done in the "Anything and Everything Goes" section and discussed it with her at the next arbitration.

"Distinguish Between Willful Defiance and Childish Irresponsibility"

"Before you discipline your children, determine their intent behind the mistakes. Willful defiance is deliberate disobedience—when children know what parents expect from them and do the opposite. This could include running away when called, screaming insults, and other acts of outright disobedience. Kids know when they're wrong and wait to see what their parents will do about it."

For willful, defiant behavior, make use of the disobeying rule. As a young teenager, Renee dressed for school in a T-shirt that I felt was inappropriate. I said, "Renee, that's an interesting shirt, but it's not suitable for school. Please go change your clothes." And she did. But after she gathered her lunch, book bag, and clarinet and left for school, I had nagging doubts about the status of the T-shirt. After canceling several appointments for that morning, I drove to Renee's school and asked to see her. I told the office staff not to tell her I was there, but just to request that she come to the office. You can imagine Renee's face when she walked into the office wearing the T-shirt.

Renee's disobeying rule said that any willful act of disobedience would result in extra chores—my choice, not hers. Because Renee was an academically strong student, I checked her out of school. On the way home, we stopped at a nursery where I asked the attendant to fill the car's trunk with mulch. Arriving at home, I told Renee to weed and mulch anything that resembled a flowerbed. She'd been defiant and I wanted the consequence to be tough.

"In contrast, childish irresponsibility results from forgetfulness, accidents, inattentiveness, intolerance, or immaturity," according to Dr. Dobson. A mom from one of my workshops related this example of childish irresponsibility: After spending a day moving into their new home, the family's teenage daughter took a break to polish her nails. As she sat on the new white couch in a formal living room with matching carpeting and drapes, the daughter vigorously shook the red nail polish bottle. Somehow the top of the bottle flew off and polish spread on the wall, drapes, sofa, and carpet. Willful, defiant behavior? No. Just a kid acting like a kid.

"When Defiantly Challenged, Respond with Confident Decisiveness"

"There's nothing more destructive to parental leadership than for a mother or father to disintegrate during a struggle. Keep your emotions under control."

My friend Dave cued me to the effectiveness of responding decisively. Several years ago he was badly injured in a serious automobile accident. Dave said his most vivid memory and the most important factor to which he attributed his survival was the paramedic who never left his side. The calm manner with which the paramedic spoke and the decisive way he took charge told Dave he was going to make it. Later, when I found myself in a crisis situation with Heather where things normally escalated out of control, I tried this technique. Instead of escalating with her, I responded with a confident, decisive voice. I also acknowledged her feelings, which validated her and what she was experiencing. Remember, it's not necessary to *agree* with the feeling to acknowledge it. You're simply putting a name to the feeling.

This produced a calming and reassuring effect that allowed Heather to calm down without feeling she was giving up control. Also, by utilizing this technique with her, she learned to appropriately cope with her anger and deal with stressful situations.

A parent's best bet?

To diffuse an escalating situation:
   1. *Acknowledge the child's feelings.*
   2. *Provide the child with a choice or alternative.*
   3. *Disengage from the behavior.*
Sample dialogue: *Respond to escalating behavior with "I can see how frustrated and angry you are and I'm sorry. I know things are bad for you right now, but I promise they're going to be better. Let's find a solution for this at arbitration."*
   Sample dialogue: *"I can see how frustrated you are and I'm sorry. But you need to set the table for dinner. Tamra, you have a choice to either set the table for dinner or lose your TV privileges tonight. I'm going to count to three, and if you haven't started setting the table, then I'll know what your choice is."*

"Reassure and Teach Your Children After a Confrontation"

Because Heather had become a master at giving the responsibility for her behavior to everyone else in the family, Dr. David Parker, our psychologist, taught us this debriefing technique. This easy technique involves asking the questions why, what, and how:

1. Why did you lose this privilege?
2. What will happen if you make that choice again?
3. How can you do it differently in the future?

Heather was required to answer the questions correctly before we would reinstate whatever she'd lost as a consequence. For example, she wasn't allowed to talk on the phone after 10:00 P.M. To do so resulted in losing the phone for a day. And when she lost the phone because she had not complied with the rule, she was required to answer the above questions before the privilege was returned. For example:

   1. Why did you lose your phone?
   "I lost my phone because I was using it after 10:00 P.M."

   2. What will happen if you talk on the phone after hours again?
   "I'll lose the phone for a day."

3. How can you do it differently in the future?
"I will not talk on the phone after 10:00 P.M."

Upon completing this debriefing technique, there wasn't a doubt that Heather clearly understood the rule, what the consequence was for breaking the rule, and more important, how she could do it differently the next time.

"Avoid Impossible Demands"

"Parents should understand their children's limitations and adjust their expectations accordingly." For example, don't expect an eight-year-old child with ADHD (attention deficit disorder with hyperactivity) to sit quietly for two hours. Or don't leave a fifteen-year-old who struggles with basic rules home alone for the weekend.

"Let Love Be Your Guide"

"A relationship characterized by genuine love and affection will be a healthy one, even though parental mistakes are inevitable." As Herb and I struggled initially with Heather's behavior, we made many parenting mistakes. But what kept the doors of communication open were the unconditional love she felt and the dignity and respect with which she was treated.

Chapter Four

■ ■ ■

WHAT THEY DO IS WHAT THEY GET

Creating real consequences and incentives

―――――――――――――――――

The beautiful antique oak coffee table was one of her most prized possessions. It had belonged to her maternal grandmother and recently, when her mother died, her father had given it to her. Consequently, you can imagine her horror when she discovered the huge scratch gouged across its top. Her young teenage son carelessly caused it when he used the table as a stand for his video game. His mother was devastated and furious. Because she wanted him to experience the pain of having something he valued damaged, she took a nail and scraped his skateboard. What did she accomplish in this? Did she teach him anything about respect for another's property or about restitution?

Why Consequences?

The goal of a consequence is to have children make choices and learn from those choices in order to shape their own behavior.[1] Therefore, when you determine consequences, always check your motive. Power, control, or revenge should never be a factor in determining consequences. Use consequences only to modify or change a child's behavior.

Unfortunately, some parents see consequences only as punishment for children's misbehavior. And tragically, for some parents the motive of teaching responsibility and appropriate behavior gets lost in satisfying their need for power, control, and revenge. Sound farfetched? How many times have you heard a parent say, "When I say jump, my kids ask how high!" Do you know of a parent whose immediate response to every request is no? Have you heard stories about people who retaliate, like the parent mentioned above?

Don't let any of that be true for you. Your motive for implementing consequences should be to deter, change, modify, or reinforce your children's behavior. This will encourage learning and cooperation between you and them. And it teaches the important distinction between acts of "discipline" and "punishment."

Discipline derives from the root word *disciple* and it means "to teach." It's a positive, proactive approach that focuses on teaching children appropriate behavior. On the other hand, *punishment* means "to chastise or correct." It negatively addresses misbehavior after it's occurred. Parents who confuse these two concepts apply a lot of punishment with little or no discipline—and everyone's unhappy. The good news is that the more you properly discipline children, the less you'll need to punish them. And it begins with the principle of "cause and effect."

"Cause and effect" as it applies to discipline (to modifying inappropriate behavior) means that every time your children don't follow their rules, specific consequences result—and without punitive comments from you. To this principle, you can add incentives. These are rewards for following rules, and they add a positive dimension to the discipline process.

This parenting technique, called behavior modification, simply rewards desired behavior and discourages undesirable behavior. This results in a behavioral change that can be immediate and lasting when coupled with helping children intrinsically identify the wonderful feeling of accomplishment and doing things right.

A parent's best bet?

1. *Identify the behavior.*
2. *Formulate a concrete rule.*
3. *Attach a specific consequence.*
4. *Follow through without comment.*
5. *Reward good behavior.*

For example, a dad I know successfully used incentives with his fifteen-year-old son who frequently skipped school. This boy didn't attend classes for more than two weeks without missing a day. The father and son fought continually, especially about the son's driving privileges, which were nonexistent because of the truancies. The family seemed locked in a conflict it couldn't resolve.

Fortunately, the dad eventually stepped back and identified the behavior he desired from his son: he desperately wanted the teen to stay in school. After this, he considered what it would take to accomplish his goal and utilized the cause-effect-incentive approach. At arbitration, he and his wife established this rule: "You must attend all of your classes at school every day. If you skip any classes during the week, you'll be grounded for the entire next week, including the weekend. If, however, you attend all of your classes every day for two weeks, you can get your learner's permit. For every day after the two weeks that you attend all of your classes, we will give you an hour's practice driving time on the weekend." Additionally, his dad provided plenty of praise, encouragement, acknowledgment, and appreciation, and focused daily on his son's success.

When I last talked to his parents, the son hadn't skipped school in a month and was turning around his academic performance. He'd also obtained his driver's license. With the cause-effect-incentive approach to consequences, you can modify your children's behavior, give them real incentive to change, and help them identify the feeling of successfully doing things well.

DIFFERENT TYPES OF CONSEQUENCES

Dr. Rudolf Dreikurs developed the concept of natural and logical consequences.[2] Both of these are very effective and frequently utilized with behavior modification or the cause-effect-incentive parenting approach.

A natural consequence is one that takes place with no parental intervention; for example, a child going hungry after forgetting to take her lunch to school. Logical consequences require parental intervention and are related to the behavior; for example, if a child doesn't put his bike in the garage at night, he will not be able to ride it the next day.

Parents also can utilize a child's leverage points when determining consequences. A leverage point is anything a child holds dear, really wants, or can't stand to lose. Because leverage points vary from child to child, consequences for the same rule may vary among children. A working consequence for not completing daily stuff by a specific time might be the loss of the phone for one child and the loss of the TV for another.

Often what works best are logical consequences that utilize a child's leverage points.

THREE SIMPLE CONSEQUENCE COMPONENTS

If possible, consider three components when formulating consequences. The first involves something the child values. Parents can determine those things simply by identifying a child's leverage points. Ask yourself: "Where does he spend his time?" "What does he like to do?" "What does he value?" One child loved to play with friends after school. Hence, losing that privilege would make an excellent consequence.

Second, teaching is also an important consequence component. An excellent way to accomplish this is by using the debriefing technique explained on pages 44-45. Another effective teaching method is requiring kids to write short essays related to the problem behavior. One mom had her daughter, who had purchased a fake ID, research and document the legal ramifications of possessing fake identification. She then required her daughter to have five friends read and sign the document. (The mother felt certain that these friends also had fake IDs.)

Three Simple Consequence Components

- Loss of something the child values
- Teaching what's right
- Restitution

The third component is restitution. Children can learn at an early age that whenever it's possible, they should right a wrong. That means they should make restitution to the person they've hurt or for what they've damaged or destroyed. Recently, when a group of kids vandalized a local baseball dugout, as part of the consequence for their actions they were required to clean, repair, and paint the dugout.

OTHER GUIDELINES FOR CONSEQUENCES

Less is better: keep consequences as small as possible. When using consequences, your goal is to modify or change children's behavior. If a little consequence (losing the phone for an evening) accomplishes that, use it. Add to a small consequence (losing the phone *plus* losing the TV for an evening) or use a bigger consequence (being grounded for the weekend) only when the behavior warrants it.

Keep consequences short term. If you apply short-term consequences, children see an end to them and an opportunity to behave differently the next time. If a child loses the phone for a day because her daily stuff wasn't completed, she can regain it tomorrow simply by doing her chores. When a teen gets grounded because he didn't earn a 2.0 grade point average for the week, he knows it's only for the weekend. Next week he can improve his grades and keep his privileges. When kids don't see an end to the consequence or a way they can win, they quickly shut down and quit trying.

Consequences and behavior should correspond. A consequence should correspond to the transgression. Therefore, decide on consequences by determining intent first. A child who totally disregarded family rules should have a tougher consequence than one who acted immaturely or irresponsibly.

Also, consequences usually won't fit behaviors if you're angry when you establish them. Instead, take time to cool off and create the consequences at an arbitration meeting. It will give you the opportunity to examine your children's behavior and, with their help, choose appropriate consequences.

Guidelines for Consequences

- Less is better: keep consequences as small as possible.
- Keep consequences short term.
- A consequence should correspond to the transgression.

Important Point!

When using consequences, don't threaten. Instead, offer choices. Sample dialogue: "I don't want (consequence) to happen. And you don't want (consequence) to occur. However, it will be a choice you make. Please don't (break rule)."

AVOIDING THE TRAPS

As mentioned in chapter 2, after household rules and consequences have been established at arbitration, parents can easily fall into two traps: they can discuss the consequence after the rule is broken, which will usually lead to an argument; or they can simply not follow through with the consequence.

Children learn quickly how to manipulate their way out of consequences. Some common tactics include:

- Throwing a tantrum: nagging, begging, and screaming relentlessly. "I can't believe you're so mean! Why do you treat me this way? You're unfair!"
- Promising to behave: swearing to never repeat the behavior. "I'm sorry! I'll never, ever do it again."
- Threatening to misbehave: promising drastic action to avoid the consequences and to punish you. "If you don't let me attend that concert, I'll run away!"
- Reforming immediately: doing whatever they think is necessary—or even unnecessary—to please you. This tactic works the best because it inspires warm feelings and makes it tough to apply consequences. "Mom, I just cleaned my room and now I'm taking the dog out for a walk."
- Attacking when you're down: waiting until you're physically tired and mentally exhausted, then hitting with a verbal vengeance. "Why can't you be like Jennifer's parents? They're not mean to her. I hate you!"

- Withdrawing love: pulling away and punishing you with silence or absence. "I'm going to go live with Dad. He appreciates me more than you do!"
- Spreading the guilt: making you feel guilty or sorry because of a special problem such as a physical handicap or a broken home or an addicted parent. "If you weren't divorced, I wouldn't be so messed up!"
- Blaming the parent: placing the responsibility for the action on the parent. "If you bought me an alarm clock I could hear, I wouldn't miss the school bus."

When it's time to apply consequences, hang on through the manipulation. By allowing children to weasel their way out of consequences, you'll communicate that they don't have to be accountable for their actions. You could also allow them to set an unhealthy pattern of irresponsibility for the rest of their lives.

CONSEQUENCES THAT COUNT

Some parents have a difficult time determining what they can and can't use as consequences. What they usually hear from a child is "You can't take that. I bought it with my own money" or "You can't take my car. Dad bought it for me." Parents, yes you can take things away. In addition to dignity and respect, you owe your children only the four things in the box below:

Things Parents Must Give Their Children

- A roof over their heads
- Three healthy meals a day
- Clothing to wear
- Unconditional love—a great deal of unconditional love

When you choose consequences, you might want to begin with those that other parents have administered successfully. These are consequences that have worked for me and for parents from the *Parenting Without Pressure* workshops.

- Removing the TVs, CD players, telephones, game systems, or the computer from the house. More than once I've traveled around town with the TV in the trunk of my car. If you want to prohibit the use of the telephone, screen the kids' incoming calls with an answering machine. And if the family wants to watch TV, send the child who lost that privilege to her room.
- Withholding favorite items. Things like bicycles and skateboards can be taken away. One mom was surprised at the cooperation she received from her daughter by removing her cream rinse!
- Taking away allowance or lunch money. Does this mean your children go without lunch? Absolutely not. Buy large jars of peanut butter and jam, a loaf of bread, and lots of brown bags—and let the kids make the sandwiches.
- Charging money for four-letter words. Also charge money for unkind statements directed at siblings.
- Writing sentences one hundred to two hundred times. For four-letter words, require a child to write, "I will not use profanity." For unkind statements, require a child to write, "I will treat my (brother, sister, mom, or dad) with courtesy and respect."
- Writing an essay of two hundred to five hundred words to explain the reason behind a specific improper behavior. This is extremely effective for children who have difficulty verbalizing.

- Assigning extra work around the house. This can include washing all the windows and screens, cleaning out kitchen cabinets or closets, and yard work.
- Grounding children to their bedrooms, the house, or the house and yard for a day, weekend, or week.
- Grounding teens from their bedrooms. This works well for kids who like to hang out in their rooms.
- Delivering a lecture at arbitration. The topic is yours to choose and it can deal with anything from the importance of getting an education to the difficulty caused by being sexually active or doing drugs.
- Walking to or from school. If they chronically miss the bus, kids can walk to school. If children chronically get school detentions, let them walk home. (A child should walk to or from school only if it's safe and not too far.) Some schools have early-morning detentions. That means arriving at school by 6:00 A.M. This might be rough on you, but it's very effective for kids.
- Stopping transportation to an enjoyable activity such as a movie or skating. Heather learned quickly that she must treat me respectfully if she wanted me to provide transportation for a movie with her friends.
- Using a driver's license as a bargaining tool. A parent's signature is required for an adolescent to obtain a driver's license. You can also take away a teenager's license.

Again, use incentives whenever possible and make them big enough so kids will want to cooperate. Rather than a win/lose approach, give everyone a chance to win. And always remember to discuss the consequences with children prior to using them. They have the right to know what to expect before—not after—the fact.

THE MAGIC OF INCENTIVES

Positive consequences or incentives are intrinsic and extrinsic rewards that reinforce or motivate children toward good behavior. Intrinsic rewards help motivate children from within, teaching them to look inside themselves for good behavior. Extrinsic rewards grant children material rewards or privileges, motivating them to work toward things they'd like to obtain.

How Do They Work?

Incentives reward desired behavior. Some parents state the desired behavior and reward when the child complies. For example: "If you have your bath and homework completed by 7:30, you may have an additional thirty minutes added to your bedtime."

The Magic of Incentives

Intrinsic rewards:	Extrinsic rewards:
Praise	Money
Appreciation	Privileges
Encouragement	Material items
Acknowledgment	Tokens

Other parents establish a rule, a consequence, and an incentive. If the child doesn't comply with the rule, the result is the consequence. However, if the child complies with the rule, the result is the incentive. This cause-effect-reward, or rule-consequence-incentive, formula looks like this:

Rule: Daily stuff must be completed by 5:00.

Consequence: If your daily stuff isn't completed by 5:00, you lose TV privileges for that night.

Incentive: However, if you complete your daily stuff by 5:00 each day for the week, I'll add a dollar bonus to your allowance.

Intrinsic Rewards

Praise: "Wow! What a great job you did in the kitchen!"

Appreciation: "Thank you for cleaning the kitchen."

Acknowledgment: "I see you cleaned the kitchen!"

Encouragement: "I know you can do a great job on the kitchen!"

Extrinsic Rewards

Privileges: "If you get in bed on time Monday through Wednesday, you can stay up an extra thirty minutes on Thursday."

Money: Money works well with older children. For example: "For every letter you raise your grade, I'll pay five dollars."

Material items: "Every day you're ready to leave for school on time, I'll pay one poker chip, representing one dollar." Poker chips may be cashed in for haircuts, perms, shoes, and clothing.

> ## Important Point!
> *Extrinsic incentives often produce immediate results.*
> *However, never use extrinsic rewards without using intrinsic incentives.*
> *You can use intrinsic incentives without extrinsic incentives.*

To illustrate: Recently diagnosed with juvenile diabetes, ten-year-old Sara required two insulin shots daily. Unfortunately, her shots soon became a daily power struggle that left everyone mentally and physically exhausted. Wisely, her mom gave up the struggle and gave the power back to Sara. Mom intrinsically rewarded Sara with plenty of appreciation, encouragement, praise, and acknowledgment each time she gave herself an injection without a hassle. Additionally, Mom rewarded the desired behavior each time with fifteen minutes added to Sara's bedtime and a poker chip. Consequently, daily Sara could have thirty minutes added to her bedtime and weekly she could "cash in" her poker chips for either additional privileges, such as having a friend sleep over, or she could save them for material items such as school clothes.

Because intrinsic rewards work much better and the results are longer lasting, that's what a parent wants to use most of the time. It's most important that in addition to praise, appreciation, encouragement, and acknowledgment you always help a child develop competency in her ability to make good choices and have control over her behavior.

When to Use Incentives

Some parents have a difficult time with incentives because they consider them bribes. But there's a big difference between the two. Bribes are used to buy good behavior; incentives are used to teach appropriate behavior.

Incentives are best used when:

Rewarding very good (specific) behavior. It's always appropriate to acknowledge specific good behavior. For example, after the Robinsons' twin daughters sat quietly for

Rewards by the Ages

Material Items, Activities, and Privileges

FOR YOUNGER CHLDREN

Later bedtime
Trip to toy store
Trip to video store to rent movie or favorite game
TV/video/computer time
Special game with Mom and Dad
Extra story

Trip to fast food restaurant
Eat anything meal
Candy bar
Favorite dessert
Bowling with friends
Movie with friend
Putt-putt golf
Camp out in back yard

Sleep over with friends
Spend night with grandparents
Bike ride with Mom and Dad
Stickers and appreciation notes

FOR TEENAGERS

Clothes
Radio
Stereo
Shoes
Tapes/CDs
Favorite snack food
Having own room
Makeup
Room decorating
Hobby materials
Sports equipment
Additional allowance
Haircuts/perms
TV privileges

Computer privileges
TV in bedroom
Phone extension in bedroom
Private phone line in bedroom
Transportation
Driver's license
Use of automobile (separate from family's)
Use of family car
Gas money
Practice driving time

Trip to beach or lake
Tickets to sporting event
Tickets to concert
Dating privileges
Extended curfew
Sleeping late on weekends
Skating
Part-time job
Video/video game rental
Later bedtime
Tokens for video arcades
Prepaid phone card for long-distance calls

hours and politely listened to Great Aunt Gertrude's repeated childhood stories, the family stopped for milkshakes on their way home.

Reinforcing children struggling with a particular behavior. Also, it's helpful to reinforce a new behavior a child is struggling to learn. For example, when a boy channels his anger at a punching bag rather than at a person, the time is ripe for an incentive.

Nothing else is working. When you're at a lose/lose stage, you can start over by adding incentives and creating a win/win situation. Recently, a couple shared that for months their rebellious daughter had lost all privileges because of her refusal to comply with any rules. In a tug of war, they were adding on the consequences and she was refusing to budge. Because she had "shut down" completely, her parents wisely decided to start over with a clean slate. But this time they gave her a reason to cooperate by making it a win/win situation.

If she obeyed the rules for two weeks, she could have her own phone line. And for each week she complied after that, she would earn use of it for the following week. As she followed the rules, her parents diligently worked on helping her grasp the tremendous feeling of doing things right. And as her success rate grew, so did her ability to see herself as a kid you could count on!

Important Point!

Always reward incentives after the fact, never before. And because of shorter attention spans, the younger the child, the sooner he should receive the reward.

HELP FOR THE MORE-CHALLENGING KIDS

Parenting is about working ourselves out of a job. It's about teaching children the basics that equip them with the skills necessary to function well as adults. For most parents this is a pretty easy process of teaching accountability, responsibility, behavior, and consequences. Unfortunately, for others it involves that plus the patience of a saint, the endurance of a long-distance runner, and the courage of a bullfighter.

Parenting Without Pressure and the ADD/ADHD Child

PWOP works exceptionally well with ADD or ADHD children. Because of PWOP's concrete format, everyone knows what to expect every time. Also, PWOP enables parents to be consistent with discipline, to reinforce appropriate behavior, and to enhance their children's self-esteem.

What Is ADD or ADHD?

Attention Deficit Hyperactivity Disorder (ADHD) has been called Attention Deficit Disorder (ADD) and Hyperactivity in the past. It's a chronic disorder that lasts throughout childhood and often into adulthood. The exact causes of ADD/ADHD are unknown, but heredity and differences in brain structure and functioning are currently being studied. A recent landmark study directed by Dr. Alan Zametkin at the National Institutes of Mental Health traced ADHD to a specific metabolic abnormality in and around the frontal lobes of the brain (reduced metabolic activity in those parts of the brain that control movement, emotion, and attention).[3]

About 3 to 5 percent of all children exhibit ADD/ADHD. More boys are diagnosed than girls at a ratio of approximately four to one. Until recently, it was believed that ADD/ADHD symptoms were gradually outgrown and that they disappeared in adolescence. It's now known that symptoms continue into adolescence for approximately one-fourth to one-third of individuals diagnosed as children.

Students with ADD/ADHD have a much greater likelihood of academic underachievement. They're more likely to be retained, drop out of school, or have social adjustment problems because they are vulnerable to failure in academic mastery and peer relations.

Treatment intervention is often necessary. Charlene Messenger, Ph.D., stresses that a multimodal treatment of the disorder is necessary. This approach will aim at assisting the child medically, psychologically, educationally, and behaviorally. Children with ADD/ADHD don't routinely show signs of serious emotional disturbance; but if they're not properly diagnosed and treated, they're at great risk of behavior disorders, depression, and even substance abuse.

Is My Child ADD/ADHD?

Dr. Messenger notes that diagnosis often requires a combination of clinical judgment and objective assessment; and because there is a high rate of coexistence of ADD/ADHD with other psychiatric disorders of childhood, assessment must be comprehensive. It should include an evaluation of medical, psychological, behavioral, and educational functioning. Assessment typically includes a detailed history, standardized behavioral rating scales, and psychoeducational assessment. The three main characteristics of ADHD are inattentiveness, impulsiveness, and hyperactivity. ADD children are inattentive and impulsive, but lack the hyperactivity.

1. **Inattentive.** The child is inattentive and easily distracted by extraneous stimuli (noise, smells, and movement). The child has trouble following directions and doesn't complete projects. He often appears not to be listening, and to be daydreaming.
2. **Impulsive.** The child is unable to delay gratification and demands constant attention. He often is impatient for his turn, bosses other children, talks out of turn, and reacts without thinking ahead.
3. **Hyperactive.** The child is restless and unable to sit still. There is much extraneous movement, and the child often fiddles with small objects or hums and makes other odd noises.

All kids with ADD/ADHD will display a different combination of symptoms that will range from mild to severe even in the same individual. For example, one teen might have mild attention difficulties, poor impulse control, and is a nonstop talker, while another will experience extreme attention difficulties and is passive in nature.

What Can Parents Do?

Here's a list of things to start with:

Learn everything about ADD/ADHD, its associated difficulties, and its impact on the family. ADD/ADHD children are not like other children. Consequently, many parents become very frustrated when parenting techniques that worked before will not work as well with these children. Typically, ADHD children are not rule-bound, have difficulty learning from mistakes, and don't have a lot of respect for authority. Don't expect to find a quick, easy remedy.

Dr. Messenger reports that about 25 percent of ADHD children also have behavioral problems that include deliberate defiance, teasing, lying, aggression, and destructive behavior. By having a clear understanding of ADD/ADHD and its associated difficulties, parents can be more realistic with parental expectations. For example, help children cope with their difficult ADHD sibling by individually "dating" the kids in the family. Also, before engaging in family activities, role-play acceptable ways to deal with ADHD behavior.

Carefully consider the pros and cons of medication. Not every ADHD child needs medication, but it can be very effective in controlling some of the behaviors associated with the disorder. In spite of some negative media attention, medications are reported to be safe and have few side effects with appropriate use.

Take very good care of yourself and your marriage. Parenting an ADHD child is a challenge and parents often feel overwhelmed. Avoid emotional overload by effectively managing your time. ADHD children require a great deal of time. Therefore, plan your schedule accordingly. For example, prioritize, simplify, and eliminate items from your daily planner. Less is definitely better here. This might not be the time to take a graduate course in engineering, to apply for that time-consuming new job, or to host the office Christmas party.

However, take time for yourself. Develop interests, skills, and hobbies, and daily do something nice for yourself. By taking care of yourself, you're able to take care of the needs of the kids. Also, if married, focus on your relationship apart from the kids.

Finally, join an ADD/ADHD support group that can provide plenty of information, guidance, and support. CHADD (Children and Adults with Attention Deficit Disorders) is an excellent example.

A parent's best bet?

> *1. Take one day at a time. Dwelling on the future can be overwhelming. The what-ifs can immobilize you.*
>
> *2. Remind yourself that no one is to blame for your child's ADD/ADHD.*
>
> *3. Practice forgiveness. Forgive yourself for your mistakes and your child for his.*

Educate others. "I just can't understand why you can't control his behavior. If he were mine, I'd straighten him out and show him what for!" are the words heard by many parents of ADD/ADHD children—and not always from strangers but often from well-meaning family members. A parent's first line of defense is to educate others. This includes relatives, close friends, teachers, and parents of playmates. Don't hesitate to meet with your child's teacher to share information and strategies you've found effective. And be especially careful in screening and educating babysitters and other caretakers.

For example, one mom invited her critical mother-in-law to attend several CHADD meetings and provided ADHD literature and addresses of several ADHD web sites. Consequently, she was able to make Grandma a real advocate and part of the solution instead of part of the problem.

Develop an effective behavior management program. ADHD children thrive with concrete, concise, and consistent discipline. Make sure your behavior management program includes all three.

Parenting Without Pressure furnishes an objective, nonmanipulative parenting tool that enables parents to be firm, fair, consistent, and positive with discipline. It also provides a format to teach accountability, responsibility, and consequences for behavior, and it allows for easy assessment in determining what is working, what is not working, and where to go from here. More important, it enables parents to shift focus to what the kids are doing right while working on their inappropriate behaviors.

ADD/ADHD is an ongoing condition, and behavior management strategies are likely to be necessary throughout elementary grades and high school. Also, you might have to modify strategies to meet the needs of the changing child.

Provide structure. Create a structured environment by establishing order, organization, and predictability. ADHD children do best when they know what to expect every time.

Establish routines, simplify specific tasks, and organize your child's time by setting schedules. Checklists are helpful reminders and allow a task to be broken into units. Also, a checklist provides a sense of accomplishment as each step is crossed off.

Help children organize materials and possessions such as their rooms or desks. The less they have to keep track of, the better. For example, musical instruments, book bags, homework, house keys, and so on should always be put in the same place.

Use supervision and intervention. Because ADHD children are highly impulsive, they require a great deal of supervision

Phillip's Morning Routine

- Get dressed.
- Wash face.
- Brush teeth.
- Comb hair.
- Feed dog.
- Eat breakfast.

and intervention. Provide close supervision during unstructured times, such as playtime with friends, to help control risk-taking and to eliminate potential injuries. When you supervise closely, you can intervene before behavior gets out of hand. It can then be handled more quickly with praise for changing rather than with criticism for a mistake.

You can give the ADHD child a sense of control by allowing some room for decision making. Presenting alternatives from which to choose, even though the parent selected those alternatives, can provide this opportunity. For example: "Do you want to do your homework at the kitchen table or at your desk in your bedroom?"

ADHD kids have a difficult time learning from past mistakes. Walk them through it. Ahead of time, ask questions such as "What else could you do?" Afterward, ask questions such as "What could you have done differently?"

To Clean Room

- Sheets removed from bed and taken to laundry room
- Clean sheets put on bed
- Clean clothes folded or hung up
- Dirty clothes put in hamper
- Books, paper, and so on put in proper places
- Room dusted and vacuumed
- Trash can emptied

Be assertive with communication. Assertive communication involves being very clear, direct, and reasonable. Say what you mean and mean what you say every single time. When making a request, make sure you have your child's attention by establishing eye contact. Then make it brief and to the point.

Help your child understand that certain rules must be followed. It's a simple fact that some things can't or will not be changed, and it's harmful to the child, as well as to everyone else, to have constant arguments. However, some things are open for negotiation but will only be discussed at arbitration.

Use a feedback model that starts with the word "I" ("I feel . . . ") rather than the word "you" (which may feel as if you're pointing a finger). For example: "I feel frustrated when we are late to school," instead of "You made us late again."

Do whatever possible to enhance self-esteem. ADHD children often suffer from poor self-esteem. Because of their short attention spans and high energy levels, they often have trouble getting along with others and doing schoolwork. Dr. Messenger warns that these problems often cause ADHD children to see themselves as bad, dumb, or unlikable. She also emphasizes parents' power to change that cycle.

The PWOP management approach allows parents to deal with inappropriate behavior while shifting the focus to what the kids are doing right. By consistently having arbitration, you're free to simply "get along" with your child and have fun. Daily find something to do together that you both can enjoy, such as playing a sport or a game, or sharing a hobby. Also, give unexpected recognition such as putting a happy note in her lunch box or under his pillow.

When social interaction takes place, carefully plan ahead and monitor the situation.

Teach and reinforce positive social skills. Expect that you may need to teach your child the social skills that other children learn without specific instruction. Teach him how to read body language, how to give compliments, and how to listen.

Start a self-esteem book. Take a photo album and put in any significant markers of achievement such as a good school paper, a ribbon from field day, or a happy-gram from the principal.

Encourage sports and physical activity. These children need an outlet for their energy, and they need an arena to feel capable. One-on-one activities such as karate or tennis may be better than complex team sports.

Develop the habit of praising children at least four times daily. Parents can help by encouraging areas where the child is good. Emphasize the process, not the product. Look at the effort extended instead of the final outcome. This helps children focus on what they're able to control and also reduces pressure to produce a perfect product.

A parent's best bet?

1. *Learn everything about ADD/ADHD.*
2. *Use concrete, concise, consistent discipline.*
3. *Create a structured environment.*
4. *Provide close supervision.*
5. *Be assertive with communication.*
6. *Love unconditionally.*

NONCOMPLIANT TEENS

When weighing the difficulties of challenging children, noncompliant kids top the scale. All children at some point have said, "I'm not doing it!" However, they usually do it. Noncompliant children say, "I'm not doing it," and they mean it.

Simply put, noncompliant behavior is exhibited when a child breaks a rule and he doesn't take a consequence; if a parent makes a specific request, he doesn't follow through; and he disappears without permission for several hours or even days at a time.

Noncompliant children can be tough and challenging. The only success many of these kids have ever known is successful failure. They frequently feel disenfranchised from society and often seek to bolster their poor self-esteems with noncompliant or aggressive behavior.

Parents of noncompliant children are "in the trenches." In order to cope effectively, parents first must take care of themselves.

Because *Parenting Without Pressure* includes concrete behavioral management, good communication, enhanced self-esteem, and unconditional love, implementing the parenting strategy is extremely helpful. It provides a consistent, structured format to reduce stressors that set off defiant behavior, and it gives the child some sense of control by providing choices. Furthermore, it allows Mom and Dad to play hardball with inappropriate behavior while enhancing the parent/child relationship.

Noncompliant kids have a "Make me" or "I don't care" attitude. They usually fall into two categories:

- They feel they have already lost everything or are now saying, "I don't care what you do." And they mean it.
- They respond to parental authority with "You and what army are going to make me!"

Here parents want to give up the struggle without giving up the authority. Be clear, concrete, concise, and consistent with your discipline. Shift your parental focus to what the child is doing right. And eliminate the "them versus us" attitude by developing and maintaining a positive relationship with the child.

Noncompliant teens need counseling. A competent therapist can help identify and treat emotional problems the child might be experiencing. Experts estimate that as many as one in twenty American preteens and adolescents suffers from clinical depression.[4] With children that are ADHD, the number jumps to one-quarter to one-third.[5] When kids become depressed, they become irritable, act out, have temper tantrums, and have other behavioral problems. Also, conduct disorder, oppositional defiant disorder, and substance abuse are common with many noncompliant children. These children are usually found on the extreme end of ADHD behavior, resulting in kids who are quick to anger, have difficulty controlling their emotions, and lash out at those around them. Proper use of medication is very helpful here.

Behavioral Signs of Depression

- Restless
- Irritable
- Not wanting to go to school
- Wanting to be alone most of the time
- Having difficulty getting along with others
- Cutting classes or skipping school
- Dropping out of sports, hobbies, or activities
- Drinking or using drugs[6]

CHARACTERISTICS OF THE NONCOMPLIANT CHILD

There are some basic traits that some, but not all, noncompliant children possess. These include:

Feels he has nothing to lose. A child that feels he has nothing to lose has no reason to cooperate. This often happens when a parent has taken everything (activities, privileges, and material items) away as consequence and the child simply has shut down, or when the parent has little or no control and the child does as he pleases. Sadly, many of these kids also feel they have nothing to lose outside the home. They see themselves with little hope and little or no future.

The old adage says that you can lead a horse to water but you can't make him drink . . . and that's right. What it doesn't tell you is that you can make the horse thirsty! And you make him thirsty by providing something you can control and he doesn't want to lose.

Find an extrinsic incentive, something very desirable, and hold it right in front of the kid's nose. Make sure the incentive is easily obtainable and short term. Additionally, always couple it with plenty of praise, appreciation, encouragement, and acknowledgment.

Suggested Incentives Kids Can "Buy"

- Car
- Computer for e-mail
- Video games
- Phone line
- TV in room
- Transportation provided by parent

For example, Harry "bought" the daily use of an automobile with his compliant behavior. That meant he complied with parental requests and if he broke a family rule, he paid the consequence rather than ran away. Moreover, every time Harry did follow through, his parents were quick to acknowledge, appreciate, encourage, and praise the desired behavior.

Unfortunately, many of these kids feel

disfranchised from society. They tend to live for today with little or no orientation toward the future. Weave your teenager a future. Keep reminding your teen of the things he's good at and how qualities such as intelligence or creativity are of value to the world. For example: "Your computer graphics are captivating. You could design web pages!"

Longs for parental approval. As tough as they seem, these kids still long for parental approval. Unfortunately, they often perceive parental frustration and anger as rejection. Not only does this add to the "you don't care so why should I" feeling, but it also pushes the child even further away from the family. Anthropologist Ronald Rohner's study of rejected children found that these kids are at risk for a host of psychological problems ranging from low self-esteem, to truncated moral development, to difficulty handling aggression and sexuality. This effect is so strong that Rohner calls rejection a "psychological malignancy" that spreads throughout a child's emotional system wreaking havoc.[7]

With the PWOP behavior management approach, parents can diligently work on the issue of compliance by creating an atmosphere for cooperation. Also, parents can dismantle the hostility by discussing confrontational issues only at arbitration. This enables parents to work on getting along by making sure verbal and nonverbal communications are positive. More importantly, it enables parents to effectively communicate unconditional love.

Is from a family involved in a power struggle. When a parent finds himself embroiled in a power struggle with a teen, he generally will lose. Unfortunately, some parents develop a "them versus us" attitude and are going to "show" the kid who is boss. Often results are disastrous. University of Pennsylvania sociologist Richard Gelles reports that most teenagers who assault their parents were once children assaulted by their parents.[8]

Parental goals should include teaching responsibility and decision making, not obedience by control. Remember that teens are not small adults. They're children and at times will act very immaturely. Always separate the child from her behavior.

Give up the struggle without giving up the authority by offering choices. For example: "Sam, you need to turn the TV off. Sam, you have a choice to either turn the TV off or lose the use of the car tomorrow. I'm going to count to three, and if you haven't turned off the TV, then I'll know what your choice is."

Power Struggles

When a parent finds himself staring at an out-of-control kid, eyeball to eyeball, and one of you must blink, guess who blinks. You do. Why? Because the parent has the years of experience and maturity. Does it mean you have lost? No. It simply means you have chosen to disengage. And you'll simply come at it from a different direction.

Suffers from poor self-esteem. Often noncompliant children have bottomed out with their self-esteem. Dr. James Garbarino notes, "One response to feeling like a loser is to mask the feelings of failure and rejection and put forward in their place self-aggrandizing behavior."[9] They act tough to divert attention from how badly they feel about themselves. These kids are at risk because they often will go to any lengths to be accepted by their peers—even unacceptable ones. Shift your focus to what the child is doing right, and celebrate small successes. This might mean that initially a parent lowers the standard of success. For example, reward a teen for following through with the consequence rather than storming off. Or celebrate Cs (instead of only Bs) on a report card.

Self-esteem is likely to be fostered when children are esteemed by adults who are important to them. This includes treating them respectfully, asking their views and opinions, taking their views and opinions seriously, and giving them meaningful and realistic feedback.[10]

Providing anchors for children can also help them stay grounded when the going gets tough. For example, psychological anchors are found in adults who are committed unconditionally to meeting needs of the kids. This can be an extended family member, a teacher, or a mentor from the community. Ideally, these anchors are found at home. Parents should always separate the child from his behavior and work overtime to help him feel that he belongs and is accepted at home.

Is using or is dependent on alcohol and drugs. Many noncompliant children have not learned appropriate problem-solving or coping skills. Therefore, they tend to mask their feelings with alcohol and drugs. If parents suspect any type of substance abuse, it's time to take a look around. This might include going through a child's room or book bag. Privacy is a privilege, not a right. It's determined by trust that is based on prior conduct and good decision making.

Legal?

Radio talk-show host Dr. Laura said it best when she noted, "Parents don't need a search warrant, they just need probable cause."[11]

Because alcohol and drug use will have a negative effect on every aspect of a child's life, parents must deal with this first. Seek treatment immediately.

What to Watch For

Studies indicate that young people may use drugs for two years or more before their parents know it. Luis Delgado, director of Quest Counseling Centre, suggests that the following behaviors can warn you that your teenagers may be involved with drugs.

- Missing school by tardiness, truancy, or frequent sickness
- Decline in grades or conduct reports and increase in school referrals
- Decrease in energy level, motivation, and self-discipline
- Decrease in attention span and concentration
- Short-term memory loss
- Loss of interest in regular activities or hobbies
- Excessive anger, hostility, or irritability
- Sullen, uncaring attitude and behavior
- Poetry, writing, and/or artwork that glamorize chemical use
- More arguments with family members, authority figures, and/or peers
- Unexplained loss of valuables or money
- Changes in friendships and evasiveness about new ones
- Negative changes in personal grooming, appetite, and overall health

- Bloodshot eyes
- Unusual use of Visine, room deodorizers, or incense
- Possession of pipes, small containers, Baggies, rolling papers, or cigars
- Peculiar odors or butts, seeds, or leaves in ashtrays or pockets

A parent's best bet?

1. *Seek counseling.*
2. *Dismantle the hostility and create an atmosphere for cooperation.*
3. *Utilize the PWOP behavior management approach.*
4. *Discuss confrontational issues only at arbitration.*
5. *Shift your focus to the positive.*
6. *Lighten up and provide plenty of unconditional love.*

TOUGH CHOICES

Unfortunately, sometimes a parent has no choice but to implement tough consequences. This may mean involving the police and/or juvenile authorities. Legally, parents can protect themselves and their property, and sometimes it takes drastic steps for a teen to understand this.

Carefully explain the following consequences at arbitration. And always conclude with this statement: "I don't want to *(whatever the consequence is)*, and I'm sure you don't want me to either. However, it will be a choice that you make. Please don't *(break whatever the rule is)*."

When dealing with noncompliant teens, here are some consequences you can use for increasingly serious problems:

Tough Kids

- They feel they have nothing to lose.
- They long for parental approval.
- Many are from families involved in a power struggle that only adds to a child's feelings of rejection.
- Noncompliant kids usually suffer from poor self-esteem.
- They're probably using alcohol and/or drugs, and may be dependent on them.

1. Remove the bedroom door. Adolescents thrive on privacy, so this can be an eye-opening experience.
2. Remove the bedroom furniture, including dressers, end tables, and bed frames, so that the only thing left is a mattress on the floor. This consequence should be used only when you have exhausted everything else.
3. If your child threatens to run away, inform her at arbitration that the street is a dangerous place and that she may not run. If she chooses to do so, then you should do the following immediately:
   a. Notify the police and report her missing.
   b. Contact every missing children's agency in your state and provide them with a recent photograph.

   c. Tell her friends' parents that your child doesn't have permission to be anyplace other than home, and if she's staying there against your wishes, you'll press charges. (Usually kids who run away stay with friends.)

   d. Remove all the furniture from her bedroom and put her personal things in storage. Leave them there for a week after she returns.

4. If a child is using either alcohol or drugs, require random drug screenings and seek counseling. If within a six- to eight-week period, the drug screenings test positive, residential treatment might be necessary for the child. (Alcohol is difficult to catch on a drug screening, so a parent will have to watch carefully for signs of alcohol use.)

5. If a child threatens you, strikes you, steals from you, or "trashes" your home and you feel that his conduct is the result of unusual circumstances, seek immediate crisis counseling.

6. A parent can press criminal charges against a teen if the child threatens a parent's safety, strikes him, steals from him, or trashes the home. If the police officer refuses to take a report, request his name and badge number and ask for his immediate supervisor's name. Report him and ask his supervisor to file the charge. If that is not successful, call the officer complaint line. Explain that a police officer and his supervisor would not press charges even though you felt threatened. Again state that you want to file charges.

7. The worst thing a parent can do is file the charges and then drop them. Before you file charges be sure you can follow through.

8. If a child is on community control or nonsecure detention, make an appointment to see his probation officer. Establish in writing what the officer is prepared to do if the child is abusive to a parent, or violates his probation, or doesn't comply with the rules. If the child's behavior makes it necessary, call his probation officer and insist she follow through with the child's sanctions. Also ask his probation officer to notify the judge and ask that a pickup order be issued. Parents should always maintain detailed notes on the child's behavior and keep all the juvenile justice/court documentation.

9. If the child is eighteen or older and chronically acts up, tell her to leave. Because juvenile laws have changed drastically in the past few years, a parent may want to talk to an attorney specializing in juvenile law. Names of attorneys can be obtained from a local or regional Bar Association referral service.

The best consequence is the natural consequence. As much as possible, parents should allow the natural consequences for behavior to occur without interference. Allowing your teen to experience the real world can be an eye-opening experience for her. Every out-of-control teenager who thinks rules apply to everyone but him should have to bail himself out of jail, get fired for chronically showing up late for work, pay fines for speeding tickets, have charges filed when he puts his foot through a wall, or be held in contempt of court for failure to comply with the rules. By allowing a teenager to reap the consequences of his own behavior, parents teach him that he's responsible for his choices. They show him that they refuse to take on his responsibilities.

Finally, it's important to remember that not all consequences are negative. Reward good behavior or even bad behavior when it's not repeated.

Chapter Five

■ ■ ■

TALKING DOWN A STORM

Fostering open arbitration and communication

When my daughter Renee was a sixth grader, more than anything else, she wanted to attend a Valentine's Day dance at a middle school. More than anything, I didn't want her to go. The dance was at night. The school was in a rough area. I'm really old-fashioned. She was only eleven years old! Every day Renee brought up the dance. And every day I reminded her that I wanted to talk about it, but she needed to save it for arbitration.

When that day arrived, Renee's first question was "Can we discuss the dance now?" I started by defining the problem. She wanted to attend a dance I felt very uncomfortable about, and I explained the reasons why. Renee didn't say much until it was her turn to talk. Then she calmly explained that I didn't know much about dances today; that they're different than the social events I attended years ago. Then Renee did something I'll never forget. She politely handed me a list of names and phone numbers of people associated with the school. The principal, guidance counselors, teachers—they were all on her list.

"Mom," she said, "please call these people this week and ask them about the dance. Then at arbitration next week, let's discuss it again."

As I sat there with my mouth open, I realized Renee had beaten me at my own game. She'd dealt with the facts and thought them through, something I'd wanted her to learn to do. I had no choice but to do my homework and call the people on the list. And Renee was right: I didn't know much about the dance.

The next week at arbitration, Renee and I brainstormed the different options and chose a solution we both could live with. She'd go to the dance and I would volunteer as a chaperone. However, Renee wanted me to fade into the background and not embarrass her. I wasn't to wave at her or her friends, give her any eye contact, or acknowledge her presence in any way. I honored Renee's requests that night. I watched from a distance and sold drinks and popcorn.

WHAT ARBITRATION IS

Renee's school dance episode represented arbitration at its best. We held our meetings on a weekly basis. We saved our arguments until the meetings. We calmly discussed a point of disagreement. We developed a compromise that we could both live with. We entered the agreement in her workbook. We stuck to it.

Granted, this isn't the way all arbitrations go, especially when you're getting started. But it's a goal to strive for: getting both sides to calmly discuss and resolve a problem into a win/win situation.

As I said in chapter 2, arbitration should take place when everyone's rested and feeling good. Saturday mornings work best for my family. However, you might consider one-to-one meetings with your children for several possible reasons: busy schedules make it difficult to get the whole family together at a specific time; individual kids request privacy; or you're a single parent and the kids have a tendency to gang up on you.

Arbitration

. . . is simply a family meeting. You can call it a family meeting, an arbitration, a family council, or any other name that suits your family.

For example, Harvey, a single dad of identical twin teenage daughters, found that at arbitration he was no match for the two together. What one couldn't think of, the other could, and they easily manipulated their way around household rules, guidelines, and boundaries. He corrected this by conducting arbitration separately. He dealt with specific problem areas with the specific twin at her specific time.

The important thing is to establish a set time and place for arbitration, to give it priority, and to stress its importance. It often works well to conduct arbitration at the kitchen or dining room table. Kids stay focused more easily if they're sitting in chairs, looking at their parents. Also, you can stress the importance of arbitration by turning off the TV, radio, and CD player, and letting the answering machine pick up phone calls.

It's also important to be consistent in having arbitrations, especially when there are no heavy-duty items to discuss. In addition to resolving conflicts, arbitration can prevent them. It's an excellent pressure valve, allowing parents and children to address small issues before they grow into big problems. This pressure-valve aspect functions when you meet regularly, no matter the circumstances.

The Arbitration Format

There's no right or wrong format for arbitration. Some families are less structured and allow kids to "chair" individual meetings. Other parents always run the show. The importance is to keep enhanced communication and problem solving at the heart of arbitration.

Should there be a time limit? Most family meetings work best if there's a time limit. Thirty to forty-five minutes usually is ample time for arbitration. However, provide the child with as much time as necessary to be heard and understood. This is especially important when coping with a challenging child who throughout the week has heard you say repeatedly, "Save it for arbitration."

What about agendas? An arbitration agenda is simply a list of those things family members want to discuss at the family meeting. Parents can either post the agenda on the refrigerator so that it's accessible to all family members or list it in the "Anything and Everything Goes" section of the child's workbook. Agendas are especially helpful if the family has a difficult time staying on track during discussions. It also allows you to think carefully about important issues and decide in advance what needs to be said and how you're going to say it. What's more, it provides a starting place for using the arbitration worksheet when tackling tougher issues.

Arbitration Provides . . .

A time when everyone is given a fair and safe platform to be heard and have needs addressed. Every family member is given the opportunity to clear the air and voice hurts and complaints without fear of repercussions.

For example, the Allisons, a blended family with five teenagers, used arbitration as an opportunity for their kids to air their many grievances and resolve differences. It also ensured that everyone—even the most timid—had a voice and a chance to be heard.

An opportunity to formulate rules and consequences. Arbitration provides a constructive format to formulate rules and consequences. Also, it gives kids the opportunity to participate in the process. Therefore, they're more likely to take ownership of it.

For example, Matt Hand, father of a fourteen-year-old daughter, found he was more consistent in following through with rules formulated at arbitration. Matt stated, "Before, I'd get angry, impose an unrealistic rule, and ground Betsy for a month. She'd cry, I'd feel guilty, and then I'd give in. However, rules formulated only at arbitration were ones not made in anger. They also required some thought and allowed Betsy's input. And now, the guilt is gone, I'm consistent, and my follow-through is great!"

An opportunity to determine operating boundaries. Parents determine a child's operating boundaries (made up of privileges and responsibilities) by his age and conduct. Arbitration provides a weekly format to readjust operating boundaries by assessing behavior as reflected in the workbook.

Case in point: With her good behavior, fifteen-year-old Dommique "bought" shopping time at the mall with her friends.

A time to compromise. Adolescents need to accept limits, but they also must learn to compromise. If you're rigid and inflexible, they'll never learn to come up with alternatives. Pick your battles carefully and compromise as much as possible. However, final decisions always rest with you.

For example, after attending private school for nine years, Marcus, who was ADD, wanted to attend a public high school with his friends. Although hesitant, his parents allowed him the opportunity because of his good record of behavior. However, they agreed to carefully monitor his progress. And if he experienced any difficulty, he would go back to private school.

The only time parents accept the challenge to do battle with a child. For the remainder of the week, the content of the workbook stands. In tackling confrontational issues, it's best to follow the "Arbitration Worksheet" (see page 147). It allows parents to stay on task and effectively work through problematic areas. It also teaches kids to logically address problems.

To illustrate: After weeks of badgering his parents for permission to attend a rock concert, Brandon finally caught on that the issue would be

Important Point!
There isn't a problem with having a problem. There is, however, a problem in not doing something constructive about it.

addressed only at arbitration. At arbitration, he came prepared with concrete facts about the concert, examples of his good behavior, and cool Uncle George as a suggested chaperone.

WHAT ARBITRATION IS NOT!

Arbitration is not the only time families communicate. Today, good communication is vital. Therefore, look for every opportunity to talk with your kids. Attend ball games, share chores, and let your kids see you as a real person. Unfortunately, what exists in many homes is task-oriented communication. For example: "Have you finished your homework?" "Did you take out the trash?"

> ### Topics to Help You Get Started
>
> - I wish you understood . . . about me
> - I'm most proud of . . .
> - My favorite subject in school is . . .
> - The person I most admire is . . .
> - My best family memory is . . .
> - I always appreciate it when you . . .

Never use arbitration as a substitute for conversation at mealtimes. Because arbitration is a time when families often tackle confrontational issues and resolve conflicts, conduct it at another time. Make conversation at mealtime upbeat, pleasant, and free of hassles.

> ### Dinnertime
>
> If a family ate three daily meals together, they would eat twenty-one meals together each week. However, a recent survey found that 8 percent ate sixteen meals together; 45 percent ate six to ten meals together; and 29 percent ate five times or fewer together.[1]

And don't use arbitration as an emotional dumping ground for you and your spouse. When emotions such as anger and frustration go unchecked, it's easy to blame all the household problems on a challenging child.

Case in point: Arbitration for the Williamsons was a nightmare. Carrie, an only child, was a major source of contention, and her behavior was rehashed at every family meeting. Finally, the family sought counseling and realized that, like many teens, at times Carrie had an attitude. However, she was following the household rules, her grades were good, and she wasn't drinking or drugging. Moreover, her parents realized that she wasn't the problem. Instead, they desperately needed marital counseling. Unfortunately, they had used arbitration as a time to emotionally download their anger and frustration on Carrie.

WHAT ARBITRATION CAN DO FOR THE FAMILY

Weekly meetings. A workbook for each child. Negotiating rules and boundaries. At first, family arbitrations sound like a lot of work. However, if you keep at it, arbitrations will easily turn into a regular family routine that you and your kids appreciate. Here's what arbitration can do for you and your family.

Eliminates everyday skirmishes. Arbitration is the only time during the week that you discuss confrontational issues and the workbook's contents. It's also the only time you establish rules and renegotiate boundaries. With these guidelines in place, the kids can't force you into quick decisions or badger you into caving in. Rather, you can clearly think through issues without making mistakes that cause you to backtrack later. This is especially helpful during a family crisis. Arbitration provides a safe setting to discuss important problems without escalating the situation. And it eliminates repeated discussions about the same problems.

Improves your home's emotional atmosphere. Arbitration is the only time during the week that you accept the challenge to do battle. Translated, this means arbitration is the only time you argue with your children about confrontational issues. The rest of the week you work at getting along with each other.

Does this mean children automatically follow through with consequences and wait until arbitration to complain about issues? Unfortunately, no. As parents, most of us have allowed kids to hook us into arguments by ranting and raving. Inadvertently, we've taught our kids that if they nag long enough, we'll cave in and they'll win.

With an established arbitration time, you can reteach kids that "I say what I mean and mean what I say" will always apply. Your response to the nagging can be "I can see that you're really upset and I'm sorry. But we'll discuss it at arbitration." This may prove difficult initially, because in many homes the destructive pattern of daily warfare has long been established. However, a change can be accomplished if parents remember that it takes two to have an argument.

Establishes routine accountability. Some kids can be masters of deception, and their parents never feel sure of what they're doing. A weekly arbitration can eliminate this uncertainty when you and your kids sit down and examine the facts. That leaves no room for surprises. When I felt uncomfortable about a situation with Heather and asked for an explanation, she sometimes replied, "Later, Mom. I gotta go!" At arbitration, she couldn't go anywhere, and I'd ask for a detailed explanation. We stayed at the table until she answered satisfactorily.

Two Points to Consider When Asking Questions

1. Never ask questions to which you already know the answer. Often this only compounds the issue by taking the focus off the original problem.

2. When asking questions, begin with the words where, what, when, who, and how. This eliminates one-word answers and opens up the conversation. For example: "How are you planning to coordinate your school work, football practice, and new job?" "When are you going to repay the five dollars you borrowed?" "Where exactly did you go when you and your friend skipped school?" "Who were the kids I saw you with at the mall Friday?"

Builds a constructive avenue of communication. In a way, arbitration can help you talk down storms rather than stir them up. It's an excellent time for family members to clear the air and say what's on their minds. This type of constructive yet emotional outlet can help family members understand each other better and tear down mounting barriers among them.

For two years, Heather used arbitration to talk to Herb and me about how miserable she felt. We gave her this weekly platform because she needed to express her feelings and know that we'd heard her. Hence we were able to communicate our interest, love, and concern, and to validate her feelings of self-worth.

Likewise, learning how to communicate constructively and effectively translates into the classroom. Students do better in class if their parents encourage open discussion at home. Arbitration provides that opportunity. According to Dr. Delores Curran, "Children need practice in expressing their thoughts before they can feel comfortable in doing so outside the home. When parents show respect for their opinions, children become unafraid to submit original and independent ideas rather than waiting to agree with the herd."[2]

Teaches problem solving. Basic problem solving is a learned skill. Arbitration also allows ample opportunity for teaching basic problem solving that encourages children to reason and think. This is especially helpful for siblings who are constantly fighting.

For example, the Martins' two teenagers constantly fought over the time each spent on their shared private telephone line. Because of this, each was required to describe the problem as they saw it and list at least two options that could be used as a solution. As a result, they decided with parental approval that they would pay for call waiting and establish a twenty-minute time limit on calls if the other sibling wanted to use the phone.

Gives parents an opportunity to lecture. Lecturing has gotten a bum rap. Typically, we think of lecturing as a time when parents provide a lengthy monologue and a kid's eyes glaze over. But lecturing is much more than that. Parents should continually look for opportunities to share their values and beliefs with their children. However, parents often find themselves lecturing to inattentive kids.

Arbitration provides an excellent time and place where parents have a much better chance of being heard. One dad wrote how effectively this worked for his family:

> Recently, at arbitration, my son, Destin, and I discussed kids bringing handguns to school. We talked about the danger and consequences of such acts and what to do if a friend brought one to school. We then played "What if" to imagined scenarios. Three months later when Destin found himself faced with this exact dilemma, he knew what to do and how to do it.

Avoiding Glazed Eyes

Create a dialogue by pausing often and waiting for feedback as you're explaining your point of view.

BEFORE STARTING ARBITRATION

Once you've decided to add regular arbitrations to your family life, there are a few things you need to know before you begin. The first is that you might be unpopular for a while, especially with kids who've grown up without family meetings and who are used to a loosely structured environment. As with enforcing consequences, you'll need to hang on through the initial complaints and manipulations, especially from older children. They might need an adjustment period, and their responses to arbitration will vary as much as their personalities.

Next, be sure that your family's authority figures are operating as a united front. Parenting styles are diverse, and often adults don't agree on the basics. In my family, Herb's style was, in my opinion, very permissive. I'd joke that if the kids wanted to build a bonfire in the family room, he'd go get the matches.

Before Starting Arbitration

- Know that as a parent you'll be unpopular at times.
- Make sure authority figures in the family are operating as a united front.
- Don't allow yourself to deal in generalities. Be specific in everything that is discussed.
- Always keep in mind that all consequences need not be negative. Good behavior needs to be rewarded, as does bad behavior that is not repeated.
- Work double time on maintaining a positive tone and attitude.

But in another way, I wasn't much better. I was authoritarian, and my usual response to the kids was "Because I said so. That's why!" You can imagine the fireworks when Herb and I tried to decide on Heather's boundaries. Our disagreements added a new dimension to Heather's determination to have her way.

Heather took advantage of our differences and became a master at playing divide and conquer. She knew if she could get Herb and me to argue, she'd wind up doing whatever she wanted. After several fights in front of Heather, though, Herb and I got wise. We started discussing our parental bottom line privately, away from Heather's earshot. Many times we conducted a parent-to-parent arbitration before meeting with Heather. For both Herb and me, this involved substantial compromises, but the effort paid off. We practiced a more balanced, constructive parenting style that worked well with Heather.

Beating "Divide and Conquer"

Kids are notorious for playing divide and conquer, the result of which is ineffective parenting. Typically, kids play one parent against the other in the hope that turmoil will occur and they'll be able to get what they want. If they do succeed in getting a no turned into a yes, they'll repeat the behavior to achieve the same results.[3]

For example, when Heather was a junior in high school her boyfriend moved to the beach, a considerable distance from our home. When his prom time came—you guessed it—her invitation was in the mail. She was delighted. This would be her first prom; she loved his radically cool, not too involved, single mom; and the invitation was for the prom weekend.

My first reaction was "Forget it." Herb's response, on the other hand, was "What's the big deal? Of course she can go." Boy, quickly did we conduct a parent-to-parent arbitration! Our solution? We rented a condominium at the beach for the weekend, she went to the prom, and we planned lots of family activities that included her boyfriend and his mother.

A parent's best bet?

1. Make sure you're in agreement before discussing parenting issues with the child.

2. Privately work out any disagreements.

3. Don't undermine your spouse in front of the kids. By second-guessing your spouse, you communicate that every rule, guideline, and boundary is open to negotiation at any time.

4. Don't allow yourself to get caught in the middle of a dispute the child is having with your spouse. Instead, encourage the child to deal directly with your spouse.

5. Consider counseling if you reach an impasse on your parental bottom line.

It's also important to be specific about everything discussed at arbitration. This includes not only problems, solutions, rules, and consequences, but also comments about positive and negative behaviors. Being specific eliminates misunderstandings and helps kids understand exactly what you want them to do.

To illustrate: Recently, Forest's parents became aware that this second-grader had been ringing the neighbor's doorbell and asking for the time, a glass of milk, or the local weather report. Basically, Forest just wanted to visit. At arbitration, his parents simply requested that he stop ringing the neighbor's doorbell. Forest did, only to replace it with knocking on the door!

Eliminate the Words

- Wouldya
- Couldya
- Shouldya

from your vocabulary

There's a world of difference between these two comments:
1. "Stop ringing the neighbor's doorbell."
2. "You may not ring the neighbor's doorbell, knock on the door, or visit in any way with the neighbor unless you clear it with me first."

Similarly, between these two comments:
1. "You're doing much better with your temper."
2. "I noticed how you handled yourself yesterday afternoon when your brother made you angry at the pool. You made a good choice when you dove into the water to cool off rather than hit him or call him a name."

Also, enter into the process with an upbeat attitude, keeping in mind that, just as in real life, not all consequences are negative. And as I said before, good behavior needs to be rewarded, as does bad behavior that hasn't been repeated.

One couple started the first family arbitration on a positive note when Dad surprised the group with banana splits. A single mom began with what she called "the positives." She asked every family member to say something positive about herself or himself and every other family member. What a wonderful way to begin!

GETTING STARTED

Children who grow up with the workbook and arbitrations consider it a way of life. Our younger daughter, Renee, started on the program at age eight. For several years, she thought every child had a workbook and every family had a Saturday-morning arbitration. Starting at a young age allowed our family to have the needed structure in place to navigate easily through Renee's teen years.

To Be More Specific

Avoid statements like:
- Be home on time.
- I wish you would . . .
- Please help out around the house.

Instead, use statements like:
- Be home at 12:00 midnight.
- I expect you to . . .
- Please empty the dishwasher.

Younger Children

Having children grow up with weekly arbitrations is a terrific preventive measure for future problems. Therefore, seven or eight is an ideal age for most kids to begin participating. For younger children, however, arbitration often serves a different purpose than for their older brothers and sisters. It's utilized mostly as an opportunity to enhance self-esteem and comment on good behavior. For example, one family used this time to again comment on and reinforce their child's good classroom behavior.

When to Start

A good time for parents to launch family meetings occurs when children start elementary school. For teaching compromise and the beginnings of democratic problem solving, it's most beneficial to start with this age group because they are beginning to have a sense of give and take.[4]

Because younger children have short attention spans, you can't wait until arbitration to correct inappropriate behavior. You need to address misbehavior as it occurs. In their book *Assertive Discipline for Parents,* Lee and Marlene Canter suggest an excellent on-the-spot disciplinary technique called "The Broken Record." With this approach, parents break the discipline into four parts: (1) a request to change behavior; (2) a repeated request to change behavior; (3) the offer of a choice; and (4) the follow-through on the choice. It sounds like this:
- "Please stop running in the house."
- "Please stop running in the house."
- "Either stop running in the house or go to your bedroom until dinner."
- "Go to your bedroom until dinner."[5]

Another effective disciplinary measure is "Do What I Want First." The principle: A child must complete what the parent wants done before doing what she wants.[6] For example: "Pick up your toys and then you can go outside and play." Or "Take your bath; then you may watch TV."

"1-2-3 Magic" is an excellent technique developed by Dr. Thomas Phelan to eliminate inappropriate behavior such as arguing, fighting, temper tantrums, and yelling. When a change in behavior doesn't occur after you make a request, here is what you do:

1. You look down at the child and hold up your index finger and say,
   "That's one." That is all you're allowed to say.
2. After a few seconds if no change in the behavior occurs you say,
   "That's two."
3. After a few seconds, if still no change in the behavior occurs, you simply say, "That's three. Now take a five-minute time-out."

Three counts within a fifteen- to twenty-minute period earn a time-out. To successfully implement this technique, you say absolutely nothing else. By continuing to talk, you take the responsibility for the child's behavior.[7]

A time-out is that period of time when the child who is misbehaving is isolated in a non-stimulating place. The child is isolated for one minute for each year of age (for example, five minutes for a five-year-old).

Tell your child what to do instead of what not to do. We have a tendency to visualize what we hear. If you close your eyes as you repeat the statements to avoid (to the right), you see the inappropriate behavior. Therefore, as much as possible, request a positive behavior change so that the child will visualize the correct behavior.

Making rules for young children. When you establish rules with younger children, many psychologists suggest this format:

1. Look at the child, ideally on an eye-to-eye level.
2. Appropriately touch the child on the arm or shoulder.
3. Establish the necessity for the rule.
4. Establish the rule and attach a consequence.
5. Ask him to repeat the rule and consequence to you.
6. Write it down.

This ensures that you have:

- focused attention
- removed the issue of control
- clearly stated the rule and consequence
- made sure that the child understood the rule and consequence
- eliminated the possibility of forgetting the exact rule and consequence two weeks from now, when you need it

> ## To Be More Specific
>
> **Avoid statements like:**
> - Stop hitting your brother.
> - Don't leave towels on the floor.
> - Don't lie.
>
> **Instead use statements like:**
> - Play nicely with your brother.
> - Please hang up your towel.
> - Be truthful.

Finally, because of their short attention spans, younger children need brief arbitration sessions, usually between ten and fifteen minutes. If you're conducting a family arbitration, attend to the younger kids first, then let them go play while you talk to their older brothers and sisters.

For Teenagers

Utilize the first arbitration to carefully describe the *Parenting Without Pressure* workbook. Before the first meeting, explain that you plan to give them more control over what they can and can't do, and that you'll look for tangible measures—following rules, being accountable for fun times and evenings out, completing daily stuff—to assess their behavior. Also tell them what behaviors—determined by your list of dislikes—you would like to see improved or changed. Ask them to think about these behaviors and about fair rules and consequences (if necessary) for these actions.

Some teenagers may resent arbitration and at first be defensive. This is especially true if boundaries and rules have been loosely defined in the past. Inform them gently but firmly that this is a win/win program that is here to stay.

Sample dialogue: "I know that you've been tired of how things have been going lately. And so have I. Likewise, I realize that at times you feel that I haven't been fair or that I stay on your case. Therefore, we're going to use this system to eliminate my nagging and our fighting. Also, it's going to give you more control over what you can and can't do because we're going to use simple, tangible measures to assess performance. However, there are some things (behaviors) that I've been concerned about and feel we need rules for. I'd like for you to think about them and what you feel would be appropriate rules and consequences. Also, I'd like for you to identify specific things that I can do to make things better for you."

No matter what their age, let your kids know that showing up for arbitration is not an option, but participating in the arbitration is their choice. However, if they decide not to talk at arbitration, parents can unilaterally decide on the operating boundaries, rules, and consequences. Once your kids learn that the workbook is here to stay, and arbitration is a chance to be heard and have their needs addressed, they'll settle down and learn how to make the program work for them.

After familiarizing the kids with the workbook and giving them (especially the older ones) the opportunity to think of specific areas they'd like to discuss, you're ready to start regular arbitration meetings. Before you get down to problem solving, though, take care of two important preliminaries: point to the positives and take care of family business. Like the single mom I mentioned earlier, start by asking everyone to say something positive about every family member, including themselves. They can praise general qualities or specific actions in the last week, and parents should especially compliment good behavior. Don't worry about verbal overkill. Kids can't hear enough positives!

TAKING CARE OF FAMILY BUSINESS

With everyone together in a family arbitration, you can make announcements and coordinate individual schedules. At our house, we used this time to fill out the master calendar so everyone would know about the upcoming week's activities and transportation arrangements. After arbitration, we posted this calendar on the refrigerator door. You can discuss anything from dentist appointments to the next family outing. Getting involved in the family's plans helps kids feel like they belong and motivates them to take responsibility and to constructively participate.

For example, Renee would frequently schedule appointments for the same time I was working. Consequently, this often resulted in a last-minute panic about transportation. We eliminated this problem at arbitration by discussing and listing activities and appointments a week in advance.

Take time to talk. Ask the kids if they have specific items to discuss, leaving your tough arbitration points until later in the meeting. (Once you start arbitrating difficult issues with children, it's hard to move on to anything else.) Letting children talk first allows them to freely discuss anything from the ridiculous to the sublime.

Heather once used this opportunity to exclaim, "Mom, you're making me crazy! You're always nagging me." I listened and took notes as she listed specific incidents that constituted nagging. As I examined my behavior over the next few weeks, I admitted that Heather was right: I said many things of a nagging nature.

Important Point!

Make family decisions by consensus (general agreement) rather than by voting (majority approval). Voting creates winners and losers. A consensus encourages cooperation. Taking care of business at arbitration can also prevent mishaps and misunderstandings.

After the initial shock, I committed myself to correcting as many of the "nags" on the list as possible, with interesting results. The more I worked on this "nag factor," the more arbitration (and I) gained credibility with Heather. She realized that I'd meet her more than halfway, and she opened up to changing herself.

Other kids will use this time just to talk. I frequently worked in the evenings, so many nights I wasn't available for Renee. However, she knew she had my attention for as long as she wanted on Saturday mornings. I made myself a captive audience, hanging on to every word. Consequently, Renee's arbitrations meant hearing about her crush on Tom Cruise, her difficulty with her algebra teacher, and the details of her latest argument with her girlfriend.

Because these things were important to Renee, Herb and I made them important to us. We invested a great deal of time and patience, but it was worth it. In the security of arbitration meetings, we deepened the communication with our daughter. Also, on more than one occasion, Renee shifted gears to address more weighty topics that needed attention.

TACKLING THOSE TOUGHER PROBLEMS

Leave your tough arbitration points until later in the meeting. Once you start arbitrating difficult issues with children, it's hard to move on to anything else.

The arbitration worksheet acts like an agenda for specific problem areas. Its problem-solving format helps you identify the problem, brainstorm options, and arrive at a workable solution.

One note of caution: Only those family members directly involved with the specific problem are allowed to arbitrate the problem. Then give all participants an opportunity to be heard. Finally, always keep your focus on the solution.

USING THE WORKSHEET

After these preliminaries, it's time to tackle the "Arbitration Worksheet," shown on page 79. It provides a step-by-step guide to discussing specific problems and negotiating rules and consequences.

Define the Problem

Before you bring up a problem, ask yourself these questions: *Is there really a problem? Is this an issue on which I want to take a stand? Will I need to develop a rule for this?* One

Arbitration Worksheet

1. Define the problem. _Renee wants to attend the Valentine's Day dance at school._

Can we stop here?

2. Let the kids talk. _Present list of phone numbers of people from school for us to call this week. (We will resume this next arbitration.)_

3. Let the parents talk. _We are not comfortable with dance but agree to call people on list._

4. Brainstorm possible solutions. _1. she can go to dance. 2. she can't go to dance. 3. she can go & we will chaperone._

5. Choose the best solution. _she can go and we will chaperone._

6. How did it go? _We were able to find a solution we could both live with! Great problem solving by Renee!_

mom decided that her sixteen-year-old daughter dressing in black and sporting purple hair wasn't the problem, so she let appearance go without comment. The real problems were the daughter's drug use and sexual activity.

If the answers to the previous questions are yes, then be specific in describing problems to your children. Focus on current behavior only, resisting the temptation to harp on past actions or project into the future. For example, avoid saying, "Oh my gosh! You're failing the ninth grade! You almost failed the eighth grade, and I bet you don't do any better next year!"

Can We Stop Here?

As often as possible, give your kids the chance to correct their behavior without establishing rules or consequences. Because writing out a rule for every behavior can discourage you and your children, try to stop at the request stage. That is, simply ask your children to change and give them the chance to do it.

At age fourteen, Renee had what I thought to be a liberal bedtime: 11:00 P.M. Over the months she started pushing the limit and getting into bed closer to 11:30. At arbitration, Herb and I discussed the need for her to rest, so we asked that she correct the problem. No rule, no consequence. She respected our request and got to bed on time that week. We congratulated her at the next arbitration and didn't write a rule or a consequence.

With Heather, it took years before we stopped at the request stage. With her will of iron, we couldn't affect her behavior unless we attached rules and consequences to our requests. But by plodding along faithfully and allowing the workbook to work for us, we got to that point with her as well. Believe me, when we finally did, it was wonderful!

Get the Kids' Input

After you've laid out the problem from your perspective, let the children respond, taking as much time as needed. Don't interrupt, react, or place a value on anything they say, especially if your response is negative. As much as possible, show empathy and that you're trying to understand how they feel. If children feel you've listened to and understood them, they're more likely to listen to and understand you.

Reply with Your Input

Because you already stated the problem, you can keep this brief. Simply say, "Here's how I feel about it," and address your child's concerns as well as your own. Take responsibility for your emotions by using "I" messages instead of blaming the kids for your worry or distress. Simply stated, the format sounds like this: "When . . . , I feel . . . , because . . . "

■ Describe the behavior you find bothersome. Simply describe; don't blame.
■ State your feelings about the possible consequences of the behavior.
■ State the consequences.[8]

For example: "When you run away, I feel terrified because it can be so dangerous being on the street." When kids aren't accused of causing parental emotional response, they're less defensive and less likely to tune out their parents.

Words to Avoid

Avoid using **why** followed by **can't you**, **don't you,** and **won't you**. These questions tend to blame rather than look for answers.

Also, this technique is great to use on a positive note: "When you clean the kitchen, I'm delighted because it really helps me get things ready in the morning!"

In addition to the words you use, check your nonverbal communication. Do you cross your arms? Point your finger at the kids? Sit stiffly in your chair? These negative nonverbal signals can betray your words by revealing anger and resentment. On the other hand, giving plenty of eye contact, nodding when it's appropriate, and leaning forward in your seat can communicate that you care.

Name the Feeling

Positive Feeling Words	Negative Feeling Words
happy	angry
glad	frustrated
delighted	annoyed
excited	discouraged
grateful	sad
comfortable	hurt
relieved	uncomfortable
wonderful	disappointed

Consider All Possible Solutions

After everyone expresses an opinion, explore possible solutions for the problem. List everything, even the solutions that sound silly. This is a brainstorming session, so everyone should be heard without feeling put down. Then, with all of the options on the table, discuss each one by sharing your personal responses rather than passing judgment on the person who suggested it. You can say, "I like that idea" or "I'd have a difficult time doing that."

Choose the Best Solution

With the list narrowed down, work at compromising and creating a win/win situation for you and your kids. Remember to carefully pick those issues on which you take hard stands. This will free you to say no to the important things. One teen was allowed to wear her purple combat boots, but her dad said no to skipping school.

Once new rules and consequences are established, write them down in specific terms in the workbook and read them aloud for everyone to hear. Be sure that everyone clearly understands that this rule is now in effect. Also be sure to note those areas of agreement or compromise. For example, when we agreed to allow Renee to attend the dance, we wrote it in her workbook. Later, when we had to say no to something else, we easily could refer to this area of agreement and remind her of our willingness to compromise.

How Did It Go?

Parents should take a minute after arbitration to evaluate progress. This will guarantee that arbitration is beneficial to everyone and is not being used as a gripe session.

In the end, arbitration is a basic problem-solving skill that is a learned rather than an innate process. It's the basis for good decision making because it teaches children to reason and think. Most important, arbitration can be applied to other areas of their lives. Heather worked throughout her college years, and if she had a problem that warranted a meeting with her boss, I felt sorry for him. I knew she was ready for him; I wasn't sure he was ready for her. By that time, she had become a master at problem solving and arbitration.

Questions to Answer After Arbitration

- Was every family member given the opportunity to be heard and their needs addressed?
- When dealing with problem areas, were you specific?
- Did you keep on track and stay positive while dealing with tough issues?
- Did you avoid using arbitration as an emotional release or dumping ground?
- Did you follow through on the decisions?

KEEPING GOOD COMMUNICATION GOING

Arbitration depends on good communication, but don't reserve open communication just for your weekly table talks.

Communicate in Everyday Life

Good communication flows from mutual respect, understanding, and trust among family members. When children are treated with the same courtesy and understanding that their parents give their best friends, it sends a strong message of love and support: "You're worthy of my interest and time and, although we might not always agree, I'll always value your individuality and your right to feel the way you do."

Tough to do? You bet. But how many times have you listened to a heartbroken friend recount a story told many times before? And instead of showing weariness and boredom, you listened with empathy. Do your children deserve any less? Kids need to be heard.

Allow Children to Speak Their Minds

You can accomplish this by valuing what they say, even though you don't agree with it. With Heather, I had to learn the difference between "valuing" and "agreeing." We disagreed on many issues, and it was a relief to realize agreement wasn't necessary. Our lack of agreement didn't automatically make one of us right and the other wrong; it just meant we held different viewpoints. Knowing this, it became easier to value Heather's thoughts and eliminated my need to win her over to my side.

The change in my attitude produced an unexpected side effect, too. When we did deal with issues that were clearly "right" or "wrong," Heather was more likely to understand my point of view when she didn't need to defend hers. Kids need to be valued.

Share Yourself with the Children

Let your kids see you and your spouse as real people. Spend unstructured time together. Attend ball games. Share chores and hobbies. Talk about all kinds of things, not just issues and problems. Really care. You can't miss when you combine listening with respect, trust, and understanding. And by all means, have a great time.

One dad shared with his son his love of remote-control model airplanes. And to his delight, his son expressed an interest in flying them, too! Together they spent many enjoyable hours refurbishing and flying old planes. As a result, they had the opportunity to connect on a different level and see each other in a new light.

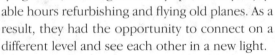

Important Point!

Don't confuse sharing yourself with using your child as a therapist or confidant. Sharing information like feelings you're having about the individual you're dating or arguments that caused your marital breakup forces the child into an interpersonal relationship that she lacks the emotional maturity to handle.

Choose Your Words Carefully

When asked, most parents will say they want good communication with their children. And yet without realizing it, they're the greatest roadblocks. Probably the biggest reason is our pressure-cooker existence today. We live with excessive stress in a fast-paced world, and the home front can turn into a dumping ground. The pressure, irritability, and exhaustion take their toll. Sadly, children end up on the receiving end of chronic irritability, abusive criticism, insensitive comments, and emotional unavailability.

Compounding this problem is the children's immaturity. Parents can lose sight of the fact that a fifteen-year-old, 186-pound boy is as close to age ten as he is to age twenty—and will act like a twelve-year-old about half of the time. Teenagers are especially notorious for responding to parental dialogue by acting bored, flip, silly, coy, or hearing impaired. It can cause parents to react with verbal blasts that emotionally cripple kids. Emotional walls are built with the bricks of thoughtless words. And trusting relationships, so longed for, never materialize.[9]

How Old Are You?

"The brain inside a teenager's skull is in some ways closer to a child's brain than an adult's. Still being forged are the connections between neurons that affect not only emotional skills but also physical and mental abilities.

"A teen's prefrontal cortex, where judgments are formed, is practically asleep at the wheel. At the same time, his limbic system, where raw emotions such as anger are generated, is entering a stage of development in which it goes into hyper-drive."[10]

A parent's best bet?

1. Don't shoot from the hip. Instead, cool off by phoning a friend, taking a walk, taking a hot bath, breathing deeply, or counting to ten.

2. Identify the source of your anger. Is it fear, frustration, hurt, annoyance, shame, humiliation, or disappointment?

3. Avoid using you're *followed by a negative adjective or noun. These words tend to attack the child's character rather than address the behavior. For example: "You're a brat" or "You're trouble."*

Contrary to popular belief, kids listen to what their parents say—and they live up or down to parental expectations. If you tell children that they're trouble, bad, worthless, or failures, they'll act accordingly. If you tell them they're important, worthwhile, and capable, they'll believe that, too. For that reason, stop and think before speaking to your kids. Say what's uplifting and encouraging so they'll share their

Comments That Build Walls Instead of Bridges

■ Playing the martyr
"I spent three days in labor with you!"
"Why are you doing this to me?"

■ Placing the blame
"You're responsible for your dad leaving us!"
"I spend so much time worrying about you, I can't hold down a job."

■ Name calling
"You're pathetic . . . really worthless."
"You kids today are such weirdos."

■ **Threats**

"Touch it again and you die."

"I'll send you back to your mom!"

■ **Sarcasm**

"That was real bright, dummy!"

"I knew I could count on you to screw up."

■ **Comparison**

"Why can't you be more like your brother?"

"When I was your age, I was a football star and never got into trouble."

■ **Criticism**

"You'll never get anything right!"

"You're a bum like your father."

lives with you. It's hard for children to trust someone who verbally assaults their self-esteem.

One parent was surprised to learn that his son felt he couldn't talk to him about being tormented by the school bully. Instead, the teen took a gun to school. But then the dad sadly realized he had "shut down" communication long ago by referring to his son as stupid, a crybaby, and a wimp. Naturally, the father was the last person the child felt he could trust.

Arbitration helps families build the foundation for positive family life. By providing parents with a practical format, arbitration can eliminate daily fighting and allow parents to clearly communicate expectations. Children learn the important skills of problem solving and good decision making. And everyone learns to recognize, value, and treat one another with dignity and respect.

A parent's best bet?

1. *Always treat children with courtesy, respect, and kindness.*

2. *Talk with your kids, not at them or down to them.*

3. *A child has a right to her feelings. Mutual respect involves accepting those feelings.*

4. *While children are speaking, don't mentally rehearse your reply.*

5. *Listen more; talk less.*

6. *Don't interrupt when your children are speaking.*

7. *Listen actively by repeating back your child's feelings with empathy and understanding.*

8. *Be available.*

9. *Make sure your nonverbal communication is positive.*

10. *Cool off before you talk. Remember, if you want to be listened to, you first must listen.*

Chapter Six

■ ■ ■

TOTS AND TEENS

Is there really much difference?

If you've experienced life with a two-year-old and now have the privilege of living with a teenager, you'll have to agree that there doesn't seem to be much difference! Both can be extremely negative and rebellious as they experience turbulent changes in their quest for identity and independence. By understanding the dynamics of the many physical and emotional changes occurring with adolescents, however, parents can often help calm the stormy seas of their fantastic rite of passage into adulthood.

To better understand teenagers, many parents draw from their own experiences as young people. For the most part this can be a mistake, because their memories tend to be distorted. Some recall the teen years as being packed full of carefree experiences. For others, it was more like a ten-block walk to school, through sleet and snow, carrying thirty pounds of books. Whatever the case, parents tend to remember those "Wonder Years" as either perfect or having been handled perfectly well.

The problem, of course, is that parents often can't grasp the reality of how it is for their kids, because their focus is still on how it was for them. It can be frustrating for a teen to be continually measured by Mom and Dad's experiences, which often produce unrealistic standards.

It's easy for a teenager today to be overwhelmed and frightened by the reality of his world. Tragically, some kids must contend with things at home such as divorce, poverty, abuse, and neglect.

At school they don't fare much better. Not only must they struggle to pass English, math, and science, but many must also cope with drugs, violence, and sex among their peers. Unfortunately, many of these same kids are confronted with either being ignored or being ridiculed and shamed by their classmates.

Because insecurity runs rampant on school campuses, kids can be very vicious. To make themselves feel bigger and better, they verbally attack anyone they perceive as different. A child can easily find his dignity stripped and his self-esteem badly damaged.

School is a child's workplace. However, his choices are very limited and in most states he can't quit until he's sixteen. One hundred eighty days of the year, school is a place he must go and contend with whatever he finds.

Fortunately, for most children school is a positive experience that equips them with the tools to lead full, productive lives as adults. However, for too many others, school is disastrous. In the corridors and classrooms these kids are often forced to negotiate emotional mine fields without adequate coping or problem-solving skills. When coupled with immaturity and lack of experience, trouble is almost sure to follow. Examples of this were clearly seen at high schools in Pearl, Mississippi; West Paducah, Kentucky; Jonesboro, Arkansas; Springfield, Oregon; and Littleton, Colorado.

Many times parents fail to realize that it's important for children to feel good about themselves. Too often parents trivialize some of their children's painful experiences. The exercise that follows might help you understand more clearly how some kids end up feeling after a school day.

Imagine

Imagine it's tomorrow morning and you're getting ready for work. As you stand in front of a full-length mirror, you carefully examine your reflection. You start by studying your hairstyle. You scrutinize your face, inspecting your eyes, ears, nose, and mouth. You examine your body frame, your weight, and look at the size of your hands and feet.

As you continue to stare at the mirror's reflection, you begin to think about your job and the particular tasks you perform. Now imagine that when you get to work you're ignored. Even though you were out sick for several days, no one realized you weren't there. People walk around you, look at you, and maybe even speak to you if it's necessary, but they really don't see you. You're never sought out for advice and never included in office gossip. No one asks you to go to lunch. You find that you're a nonentity. How do you feel?

There is one thing worse than being ignored, however.

Imagine that you find your particular job very difficult. Even though you honestly try, you're often ridiculed because sometimes you do your job poorly. When you make a mistake, it's quickly pointed out by someone who implies to your coworkers that you're a real slow thinker or maybe even just plain stupid. Someone might even suggest you're slightly retarded. In fact, they make Retard your new nickname. The office staff loves this because your inadequacies provide them with a good time for those long afternoons.

Also imagine that even though you carefully dressed for work, the office fashion critic is all too quick to point out to the others that your clothing doesn't match, doesn't fit, isn't in, or isn't very expensive. In fact, what you have on could be considered a real Goodwill special. You're deemed a real nerd. When the crowd doesn't call you Retard, they call you Goodwill Special.

Now think about your hair and imagine that someone asks, "Did you do that to yourself or did a lawn mower run over your head?" You're also likely to hear, "And you actually wear glasses? It's obvious you don't realize that glasses make your nose look soooooo big and your ears stick out! Also, you really need braces. And by the way, is that a pimple or a mole?"

Finally, imagine that the comments turn to addresses, and yours is discussed at great length. Everyone knows that living in that area of town must mean you're poor, which means that you're less than important. If your address doesn't reveal your all-too-important financial status, your car will. Some coworkers can't believe you actually have the nerve to be seen in something so archaic. What a relic! But then, that's what they expect coming from a family like yours. The conversation ends when someone asks, "Why did you even bother to come to work today? This place would be better off without you."

Does this exercise exaggerate the point? Somewhat, but if you listen carefully to many young people today, you'll realize that this illustration is not far off. Unfortunately, when comments such as these are heard often enough, they gain credibility in the mind of a young person. When teenagers are asked today to describe the popular kids in their schools, they talk in terms of money, looks, and brains. If a child happens to be missing one or all three and he doesn't happen to be a star athlete . . . watch out!

CHANGING IN THE HALLS

While kids are trying to cope with these ridiculous standards of measurement for their self-worth, they're also undergoing tremendous physiological and emotional changes. The wonderful time in life known as puberty is responsible for these drastic changes.

Puberty is occurring at an increasingly earlier age. The average age for menstruation for girls in the United States is twelve and a half. During this time, energy levels of a teen will dramatically fluctuate because of the continual hormonal changes. A child can be full of energy one day, only to suffer from extreme fatigue the next.

Due to a teen's increased metabolic rate, he'll experience an increased appetite and rapid growth. Watching a teenager eat a meal during these times of rapid growth can be a startling experience for parents, second only to trying to keep groceries in the house.

The physical growth experienced by a teen during this time will be unparalleled except by the first two years of life. For example, it's not unusual for a child to grow five inches and gain twelve pounds within a year. Just when he becomes somewhat comfortable with the way he looks, he's suddenly faced with another spurt in growth that adds inches and pounds. Different parts of the body grow at different rates because this explosion of growth doesn't follow a consistent pattern. For example, a child's arms and legs might grow faster than his backbone. Consequently, the child who could move effortlessly through the corridors at school one day suddenly finds himself stumbling over his feet the next. And the clothes that fit last month become tight as the bathroom scale records another pound or two.

Teens spend endless hours examining their reflections as they search for any flaw or imperfection that wasn't there yesterday. The questions they most frequently ask are "Am I getting fat?" "Does this really look all right?" "Am I too tall (or too short)?"

One of the cruelest jokes Mother Nature can play occurs during the early teen years, when kids are their most insecure. To compensate for their insecurity, young teens long to be carbon copies of one another. Yet the biological clocks of adolescents are not synchronized. This can cause havoc for a young girl who develops much earlier than the other girls and finds herself heads taller than everyone in the class except the teacher! Or still worst is the ninth-grade young man who still looks like a twelve-year-old and sounds even younger.

Knowing what to expect eliminates the element of surprise when these physiological changes take place. And it enables parents to prepare children for the many accompanying emotional changes as well.

Changes to Expect in Teenagers

- Extreme mood swings
- A struggle for independence
- A search for identity
- Peer group importance
- Self-centeredness and instant gratification
- Heightened sexual awareness
- Fragile self-esteem

Extreme Mood Swings

Because of a teen's tremendous hormonal changes, his emotional state is unpredictable, to say the least. Author David Veerman summed it up nicely when he said, "A teen's behavior is like the weather in Chicago. If you don't like it, wait around a minute and it will change."[1] Parents can easily become bewildered, confused, and exhausted as their child rapidly goes through his entire range of emotions. Although these highs and lows are expected, they can exasperate parents.

Often these extreme mood swings are referred to as a teen's roller coaster of emotions. This term best described what Heather often experienced. She would be happy and laughing and then miserable and crying within seconds. Unfortunately, it was some time before we learned to stay off Heather's roller coaster. On more than one occasion, my entire family's temperament was determined by fourteen-year-old Heather's emotional state.

During this time Heather displaced much of her anger and unhappiness. She was often miserable and was convinced we were responsible. Many times I found myself caught up in her moods and would take personal responsibility for them. I spent fruitless hours trying to appease her. Years later I finally learned not to take responsibility for Heather's emotional state. And by detaching myself from it, I no longer took her conduct or comments personally. Instead I concentrated on being a constant in Heather's continually changing emotional state, the anchor she could hold on to.

A Struggle for Independence

A child needs to move away emotionally from her family before she can ever move away physically. Unfortunately, this can be an eye-opening experience for Mom and Dad. Until the teen years, the family has been the dominant group the child has drawn her identity from, and most parents bust their buttons at this.

Imagine the surprise parents feel when, around age twelve or so, a daughter no longer wants to be Dad's little girl and has struck out on her own—or at least has gone as far as the nearest peer group. During the teen years, it's this group that a child usually looks to as she struggles to put some distance between herself and her family.

Putting this distance between the child and her family is usually accomplished in several ways. One of the most common is for the child to make a statement with her clothing—usually by dressing very differently from Mom and Dad. The results are interesting, with kids wearing everything from micro-minis to saggy pants!

Seeking out parental flaws and self-righteously giving the parent a detailed report is another way a child puts some distance between herself and her family. Heather was great at this. For example, she would continually compare me to all her girlfriends' mothers: "I can't believe you're about the same age as Sally's mother. She's so much younger looking! You really should have her teach you how to dress. Her clothes are so hot!" "Get with it Mom. Your hairstyle went out ages ago." "You're not going to wear those shoes again, are you? They look so dumb!" On and on she would go. At this point, tough as it may be, try not to be resentful, exercise patience, and be the very best support mechanism possible as the child moves away.

Many teens experience ambivalent feelings about being independent young adults. Often they struggle with the conflicting feelings of wanting to be a little child again and desiring total independence, all within minutes. These mixed desires can be very bewildering for kids and can leave parents totally confused. Again, be patient with your teens' struggles as they try to figure out who they are apart from the family.

A Search for Identity

This is a time when kids try to discover who they are and to formulate thoughts, feelings, and attitudes that are uniquely their own. Developing an identity separate from the family is a slow process that at times can be challenging.

This stage of life is much like a child going into a stranger's closet and trying on all the clothes. He isn't sure what he likes until he can see how it looks and feels on him. And just because he happens to have something on one day, that doesn't mean he'll wear it for a lifetime. Thus, kids will have purple hair one week and a buzz haircut the next.

The adolescents of the 1960s best depicted this process. The parents of this group of young people were a very conservative lot. Dad, having just fought in World War II, did two things his father probably never did. With financing from the Veteran's Administration, he bought his own home. And with the GI Bill paying his way, he went to college. The adjective most frequently used when describing a good husband and father of this era was simply "good provider." Dad worked long and hard, and both parents placed a high value on hard work and education.

You can imagine the excitement generated, therefore, when their children hit the adolescent years and began questioning and experimenting with the values and goals of their parents. Yes, this was the group that put flowers in their hair and hitchhiked to San Francisco. Mom and Dad went ballistic. What happened to those kids and where are they today? Take a look around. Many of them are probably your neighbors and friends who have MBAs, stock portfolios, and expensive cars.

During this time of change, the very worst thing a parent can do is panic and start to use labels. Continually saying to your teen, "You're just a punk!" might be the very thing that convinces her that she is. Be sensitive and tell your children you love them not because of what they're wearing but because of who they are.

Peer Group Importance

During this time, peer groups take on considerable importance. When a teen first starts to move away from the security of the family, he's still far too fragile and vulnerable to stand alone. So he'll look to his peer group for the guidance and support he needs. By watching his friends, a teen learns how to dress, dance, talk, and—unfortunately at times—even how to act. This is a time for testing values, attitudes, and feelings, and for experimenting with all of these and more.

This peer group will offer a sense of belonging and provide ways to be admired and accepted. It also will become a learning laboratory. By watching his peers, a teen can develop new social skills such as compromising, negotiating, and interacting. And finally, from this peer group will probably come his first opportunity to date.

Having a child influenced by a negative peer group is every parent's nightmare. Often in an attempt to protect kids from danger, parents resort to desperate measures that usually include grounding the child for life and telling him his friends are rotten people. Both are sure to backfire. Yet what's a parent to do?

It's important for parents to remember that children want to be listened to, taken seriously, and loved unconditionally. They also have an incredible need to feel they belong and they count.

As a parent, your first line of defense is to make sure your child is getting all of these things at *home!* Work hard on building a relationship with your child. Listen without being judgmental and ask him for advice or for his thoughts on a particular subject. More important, even if you don't like his *behavior,* make sure you communicate your unconditional love and acceptance of *him*.

Additionally, remind your child that he's capable of making good choices, and when he's in doubt about participating in some group behavior to simply ask himself these questions: Is this illegal? Is this immoral? Is this something I shouldn't do at this age? Could it hurt me or anybody else? Could it make a difference in my life in five years? If he can say no to those questions, he probably will be okay. Also remind him that if he's still in doubt about doing something, he can always ask you or someone else he trusts. And let him know that you can always be used as an excuse: "I want to, but my parents would ground me forever."

Finally, because peer groups are very influential, parents should take whatever steps necessary to maintain positive friendships with good kids. Early in a child's life, parents should do whatever is necessary to expose their kids to positive peer groups.

A parent's best bet?

1. Keep the kids on your turf. Create a pleasant and friendly environment, and encourage your child to bring his friends home.

2. Lighten up as much as possible. However, remember it's your home and you have a right to set a standard of conduct for your home.

3. Warmly greet your children's friends and always treat them with courtesy, kindness, and respect.

Coping with Undesirable Friends

If a child's friend is totally unacceptable, and you know that if you forbid future contact your child will grant that request, go ahead and forbid it.

Unfortunately, that rarely occurs. Frequently, such requests result in a clandestine relationship between your child and the friend, and you don't have a clue as to what is going on. Instead, restrict where, when, and how time is spent with the friend. Then structure it so that time spent with this kid is on your turf with your supervision.

Remember, criticizing a child's friends often backfires because it puts your child on the defensive. She then usually defends her friends at all cost and hangs on to the relationships for dear life. Instead, don't criticize her friends, and formulate clear rules pertaining to friends that include:

- The friend can't be more than two years older.
- The friend must be in school. Studies show that friends have a powerful affect on a child's school performance.

Why Not Older Friends?

According to a recent Alan Guttmacher Institute study, 66 percent of all teen mothers had children by men who were twenty or older. In many cases the age spread was three to four years. However, the younger the girl, the older the guy.[2]

Self-Centeredness and Instant Gratification

Teenagers can be extremely self-centered and demand immediate gratification. They can easily become consumed with themselves. Much of this is because of the rapid changes they're undergoing, especially during early adolescence. They never quite get a chance to grow comfortable with the way they look before they've changed again. Therefore, *me, myself,* and *I* are favorite pronouns.

Adolescents become obsessed with what they're going to wear, how they're going to fix their hair, what they're going to say to this person or that person, and so on. And because they're so obsessed with themselves, they're usually convinced everyone else is as well. An example of this occurs when a teenager tries on everything in his wardrobe trying to determine what to wear the next day at school. Or when a teen announces that his life is ruined because of a pimple on his chin.

Parents can help kids learn to look outside themselves by fostering a child's empathy, tolerance, and sensitivity to others by reinforcing unselfish behavior. And as a family, talk about how others might feel in various circumstances. Practice giving your time and talents to others. And always acknowledge, praise, appreciate, and encourage all efforts.

For example, before opening gifts on Christmas morning, the Giffords serve breakfast at the homeless shelter, and during the summer they volunteer two weeks to work for Habitat for Humanity.

For many teens, these years are a time of immediate gratification and instant results. Unfortunately, this doesn't necessarily get better as they get older. Because they see it happen on TV all the time, they believe every problem can be solved in thirty minutes with two commercials, or one hour with four commercials if it's a really serious problem.

Working is a great experience for many teens. It can enhance their self-esteem and teach responsibility. However, it also can add to the problem of teens experiencing instant gratification. Because much, if not all, of the money a teen makes can be used for her discretionary spending, rarely does she choose deferred gratification. It's no longer a question of saving for a new blouse or pair of shoes. If she wants something, she simply gets it immediately.

Author James Gardner suggests, "The teenager's frequent need for immediate gratification seems to be a leftover childhood tendency simply not yet outgrown."[3] The ability to postpone gratification is one of the major marks of maturity. Parents should start early in developing this area of their children's maturity.

Heightened Sexual Awareness

Although statistics tell us that more teenagers are becoming sexually active earlier, most of them are incredibly ignorant about their own bodies and sexual feelings. And because much of what they learn concerning sex comes from TV, music, movies, and friends, teens often tragically confuse the concepts of sexuality, love, and intimacy. Our young people certainly deserve better.

Parents need to equip teenagers with the knowledge that will enable them to make sound choices and take responsibility for their own sexuality. Unfortunately, many parents are reluctant to do so for fear that this information will cause their children to become sexually active. Yet studies have proven that just the opposite is true.

Additionally, it's vital for parents to continually share their values, attitudes, and beliefs with their teens and to encourage them to make decisions about being sexually active before, not after, the fact. Parents also should inform their kids that not everyone is having sex. Most of the kids who say they are . . . aren't! Encourage your children to wait. Being a teenager is tough enough without the added dimension of being sexually active.

Parenting expert Dr. Kevin Leman states,

> Sex is a wonderful gift, and when used and developed correctly, it can be very beautiful. But it's not a way to build a solid, lasting relationship. The very act of sex, which can bring new life and joy, can also, through misuse, bring destruction and devastation to many lives.[4]

However, Heather said it best when as a college student she wrote to her younger sister:

> Why wait? Having sexual feelings is normal, and having them doesn't make you a bad person. However, when you act on those feelings as a young person, it's easy to lose your balance. Believe me, this is not the time for acting on them.
>
> Adolescence is a time to learn how to be friends, to trust your feelings, to take care of yourself, to be responsible, to set goals, and to discover who you are. Because things are out of sequence when you add a sexual dimension to your life as a teenager, it's easy to lose learning all these things in the sex.
>
> Also, it's tough enough sorting out your thoughts and feelings for someone when you're not sleeping with him. But once you start sleeping with him, it can prove to be an impossible task. This is because everything becomes very exaggerated.
>
> Decide before, not after, the fact about being sexually active. And then build in whatever safeguards you think are necessary to keep that commitment to yourself. Be good to yourself and wait.
>
> Love, Heather

For teenagers, abstinence is the only way to go. However, if a teen is already sexually active, telling him not to be is not going to make him stop. Only a healthy self-esteem and his decision will do that. But what is at stake is far too important for you to neglect being sure he has the information to act responsibly. That might be very hard for some parents to do, but today the risk of an unwanted pregnancy or of contracting a sexually transmitted disease has to be considered.

The following list serves as a tool to create open lines of communication about sex, as well as a reminder to parents to carefully hear what their teenagers are saying.

"I Hear" Checklist for Parents

- Be informed.
- Be honest.
- Be early.
- Be available and askable.
- Be realistic.
- Be a positive role model.

Be informed. Kids today are extremely misinformed. But guess what. So are many parents. Make sure your information is correct. When parents provide erroneous information, they often lose credibility with their teens. Don't hesitate to check your local library or bookstore for current information about the risks, responsibilities, and realities of sexual activity (pregnancy, birth control, sexually transmitted diseases). Other sources of information include your local health department, your physician, a school nurse, or a guidance counselor.

Learn the reasons kids become sexually active. Many do so because they have confused the words *love, intimacy,* and *sex.* They've traded off one hoping to get the other. Other reasons include loneliness, the need to rebel, and peer pressure. Finally, provide kids with the skills needed to say no. These include:

- Being responsible
- Making good choices
- Resisting peer pressure
- Communicating assertively
- Knowing their limits
- Not using alcohol and drugs

Growing Up Too Soon

Teen mothers are less likely to finish school and more likely to rely on welfare. Additionally, their pregnancies are more prone to complications. And their babies face a higher risk of prematurity, low birth weight, and death.[5]

Be honest. Kids need to know where their parents stand. Share your values and beliefs with your kids. Also, don't be afraid to tell your teens that while having sex is a very adult behavior, it doesn't make adults out of teenagers! Being sexually active without the emotional maturity that only years and experience develop can be—and often is—a nightmare for many young people.

Always discuss being sexually active in a larger context of building relationships based on commitment (ideally marriage), dignity, and respect.

Be early. Start early with your children. Waiting until they're adolescents to discuss sex is too late. Instead, continually answer your children's questions and provide information in an age-appropriate way as they're growing up. Provide good sex-educational books written for children slightly younger than yours so they can understand the subject better.

"Should I Have Sex?"

Advantages to not being sexually active:
- A good reputation
- An enhanced self-esteem
- Educational and career opportunities

Disadvantages to being sexually active:
- Chance of STDs
- Unwanted pregnancy
- Guilt, depression, and low self-esteem

Be available and askable. Create an open, ongoing dialogue about sex with your children regardless of their gender. Use news items, TV programs, and the radio as opportunities for discussion. Help your children feel comfortable about asking you anything! Be careful not to be judgmental in your comments or to nonverbally say, "Don't ask me that!"

Be realistic. Think about the world kids live in today and the sexual messages they're bombarded with constantly. In a year's time, a child is exposed to fifteen thousand references to sexual intercourse, with less than 150 of them mentioning birth control or abstinence.[6] Given these numbers, it's not surprising that in 1990 approximately one million teenagers became pregnant.[7] Faced with this reality, today's parents are learning that telling teens "No!" doesn't keep them from having sex. Teach your teens how to make informed choices. Make sure you are your child's primary source of information.

Inform kids that not everyone who says he is sexually active is. Teach teens strategies for postponing sexual activity, such as learning responses to these classic lines: If you really loved me, you'd have sex with me. You must be the only virgin left in school. We might die and never have another chance. If you don't want to have sex with me, you must be gay.

Advise kids that even after having had a sexual experience, they can choose abstinence for the future. Kids who feel they have a promising future are much more likely to postpone becoming sexually active. Empower your child to see hope and promise for her future. Then discuss her goals and opportunities, and brainstorm ways to achieve them.

Be a positive role model. Children learn a great deal about sexuality by watching their parents. They're significantly affected by how warmly, respectfully, and affectionately their role models treat one another. Be aware of your attitudes and feelings about your own sexuality, and make sure what you communicate to your child is positive.

Fragile Self-Esteem

Self-esteem is simply how you feel about yourself. And it's the magic wand that determines a child's success.

Important Point!

Unfortunately, the worse kids feel about themselves the more willing they'll be to conform and to buy a sense of worth by doing what everyone in the group is doing.

More than anything else, a healthy self-esteem will enable a teenager to say no to alcohol, drugs, sex, and misguided peer pressure. It will enable teens to take good care of themselves by making good choices and sound decisions.

Adolescence is a time when self-image usually plummets. Few teenagers like the way they look or feel acceptable to the opposite sex. In fact, according to a study of 3,129 middle school students, 55 percent of the eighth-grade girls thought they were fat, yet only 13 percent were actually overweight. And one out of two girls and one out of four boys had been on a diet.[8]

Unfortunately, dismay over body image starts even before puberty. About 40 percent of nine-year-old girls told researchers they feared getting fat, as did 81 percent of ten-year-olds.[9]

BEING PREPARED FOR CHANGES

Change can be frightening, especially if it catches a person unaware. This is especially true of teenagers as they first experience the many changes of puberty. A little preparation—by carefully explaining to children the many things to expect—can go a long way in preparing everyone for this transition.

Don't tease kids about physical changes. The intent might be good-natured. But teens are especially sensitive to what's happening to their bodies and are likely to interpret such teasing as a sign that there's something wrong with them. Also, look for ways to celebrate the changes they're experiencing. For example, one dad gave each of his daughters special lockets when they became teenagers.

In addition to explaining the physical changes, you might want to make a list of the thoughts and feelings a teenager will probably experience during this time. Then put a date on the list, tuck it away in a safe place, and wait. When the going gets tough—and it surely will—get out the list, note the date, and read it.

Many times during her teen years, we pulled out Heather's yellowed list and lovingly reminded her of what we'd talked about years before. And more important, we assured her that she wasn't always going to feel the way she listed on paper. Gently remind your child that the problem is not with you or with him. It's this particular time that every teenager has to go through.

Feelings Teenagers May Experience

- Nobody likes me . . . especially Mom and Dad.
- I feel ugly.
- Nobody understands or cares.
- Anyplace would be better than here.
- I feel like running away from home.
- I just wish everyone would leave me alone!
- My parents treat me like such a baby.
- I feel like crying all the time.
- Sometimes I feel like I'm going crazy.

Being Prepared for What's Normal

Let's face it. A great deal of a teenager's behavior gives parents the opportunity to develop important character traits such as patience, understanding, and a very high tolerance for frustration. Fortunately, most of what kids do is benign. However, it helps for parents to remember that although fifteen-year-old Junior is six foot four, he still is a little guy! Dr. Ross Campbell says it best:

- Teenagers are children.
- Teenagers will tend to act like teenagers.
- Much of teenage behavior is unpleasant![10]

How true! All parents of teenagers have shared similar experiences that validate this. For example, young teenage boys love to cup their hand tightly under their armpit and squeeze down forcefully with their arm, thus making a very strange noise. And teenage girls insist on carrying all their makeup, hair spray, brushes, combs, mouthwash, perfume, nail polish, every note ever written, and pictures of every friend they have had in the past five years. Somehow, all of this fits in their purses, which they periodically leave at school, in restaurants, and in the car.

How many of you know of a kid who has worn bowling shoes home from the bowling alley or left all his schoolbooks on the bus? Also, with older teens, what is the very first thing you do after you get into the car that your teenager has just driven? Right! You turn down the radio, even before you turn the ignition on!

None of these things is fatal—just annoying. But knowing what to expect, and having realistic expectations of teen behavior, can go a long way toward a peaceful existence.

COPING WITH THE FOUR B'S

Many young people suffer from feelings of inferiority. If you ask any boy or girl in junior or senior high school to describe the most popular kids at school, *beauty*, *brains*, *bucks*, and *brawn* are the words you'll hear. This can be pretty frightening for parents who believe their children are lacking one or more.

Author David Veerman lists these excellent suggestions parents can use to help their kids cope with the distorted sense of values that many teens use to measure worth.

"Don't be surprised."[11] It's normal to want to be accepted, to dress up for one's peers or a special person. In this regard, let's not judge hastily. We adults do the same thing. We follow fashion gurus religiously. Analyze your wardrobe and think about how often you check your own appearance.

"Don't condemn."[12] Parents should gently help their teenagers understand the necessity for cultivating deeper, more important qualities such as love, compassion, honesty, loyalty, integrity, and self-discipline. And parents should affirm those qualities in their children and their friends.

"Understand the problem. Our standards are all infected by society's sickness. Studies show that beautiful people tend to be favored in school, politics, and business. Our kids live with this reality—from class officers to homecoming royalty. They need to know adults struggle as well."[13]

The problem has been around for a very long time, and to some extent we've participated in it. Take a good look at the children's stories that your kids (and possibly you) grew up with. What was wrong with Dumbo, the flying elephant? His big ears! Sleeping Beauty was envied because of what? Her beauty. What happened to the ugly duckling? He turned into a swan! And finally, The Beauty and the Beast . . . the beast turned into a handsome prince, which of course meant he was good-looking and had money!

Also, take a look at the toys we buy our children. Oregon State University researcher Elaine Pedersen and her colleague Nancy Markee examined Barbie and fifteen other fashion dolls. The results were very interesting. The researchers found that if Barbie were life-size, her measurements would be 31-17-28. Waist measurements on the other fashion dolls would range from seventeen to twenty-three inches and they would be six-foot-two to seven-and-a-half feet tall. Yale University psychologist Kelly Brownell conducted similar research. She concluded that a normal-weight female would have to grow two feet in height, add five inches to her bust size, and subtract six inches from her waist to be like Barbie. To be like Ken, boys would have to grow twenty inches in height and put on eight inches in neck size and eleven inches in the chest.

No wonder many kids have a problem with their body image!

"Feel their hurt. It's easy to dismiss your child's situation as a stage or growing pains, but the pain is real."[14] To ensure that peers don't think they're inadequate, adolescents need to feel they're accepted in the peer group. This need to belong is common to all adolescents regardless of their family background, peer status, or achievements. Start by acknowledging that your child's desire to fit into his peer group is valid and important, and help where you can.

Unfortunately, in the area of appearance, I wasn't the least bit compassionate with Heather. I felt that conformity was a ridiculous measurement of a person's worth, and I wasn't going to buy into it. During this time, young girls had to have Jordache jeans. I felt that no child of mine was going to advertise a manufacturer by wearing a product that had a label or name stamped on the seat of the pants. I was firm in my stand, and for a long time Heather didn't have her Jordache jeans. Instead, she opted for safety pins in her ears and a very strange color on her hair.

What exactly did I accomplish in my stand? Nothing positive. At a time when it was crucial for her to conform, I said no to a desire that was very safe.

Clothing

Now does this mean that as parents we have to refinance the house to keep our kids in designer clothes? Heavens, no. But offer them alternatives.

Kids can become great consumers when they control the money. Develop a realistic budget and then stick to it. Then provide a school clothing allowance and teach them how to shop! If kids want expensive items, have them pay the difference from their pocket money or earnings. Never pay retail for anything. Shop at the outlet stores. (Have kids research where they can find the best bargains.) Check out garage sales for great bargains. Also, shopping at local thrift shops is a great way to save money!

Basic Hygiene

Did you know it's quite possible for a fourteen-year-old boy to shower with a bar of soap in one hand and a washcloth in the other and never get his back wet?

A parent might need to help in these areas:
1. Require a child to bathe daily.
2. To wash their hair regularly.
3. To brush their teeth a minimum of twice daily.
4. To use deodorant (for older kids).

Basic Grooming

Hygiene deals with cleanliness. Grooming is more subjective. It deals with one's overall appearance and includes everything from neatness of hair to the condition of one's complexion. A new haircut, new glasses or contact lenses, braces, or a trip to the dermatologist might do wonders for your child's self-esteem.

Personal Habits

Some habits are irritating and annoying. For example, one child scratched the back of his throat with his tongue, producing a horrific sucking noise. Help kids become aware of how others perceive them. For example, discuss how you feel when you're exposed to someone who chews food with his mouth open or doesn't cover his nose when he sneezes.

Basic Social Skills

Poor social skills interfere with relationships with parents, teachers, and friends.[15] Some children fail to pick up social cues that dictate appropriate behavior. Consequently, they may have trouble making or keeping friends. For example, they may turn kids off by talking too loudly, acting like a know-it-all, or not knowing how to take a joke. Likewise, they may brag, or be aggressive or bossy.

1. Cultivate warmth and empathy and teach kindness and respect. Linda and Richard Eyre suggest that parents let their kids see them being concerned for the property and rights of others, assisting the elderly, caring for nature, being polite in all situations, and showing self-respect in terms of how they look and how they speak.[16]

These traits are best learned by example, and kids watch Mom and Dad very carefully. Remember that how parents treat their children often becomes the basis for how kids treat others. Also, parents should reward acts of kindness. Psychologist Julius Segal points out that just as it's important to let children know how strongly you feel about their unkind acts, it's important to let them know how you regard their kind ones. For example: "I saw you take care of the boy who fell on the playground. That was very kind of you, and it makes me feel very proud."

2. Role-play social situations. Practicing social skills at home can help children tremendously. For example, with younger kids, skills such as sharing, waiting your turn, and saying no politely can be practiced through role-play. With older kids, practice how to initiate conversations, talk on the phone, or invite a friend over. Also, it is helpful to practice listening without interrupting, maintaining eye contact, and remembering to say thank you.

3. Teach children to introduce themselves to others. Learning how to introduce yourself to others is important. Maintain good eye contact, a pleasant facial expression, and a relaxed body posture, and say simply, "Hi, my name is . . . "

4. To have friends, you first must be one. If you want to have true friends, you must be a true friend. The qualities of a good friend include being . . .

- *Caring.* Shows genuine concern and cares about her friend's well-being. Remember, "Do unto others as you would have them do unto you."
- *A good listener.* Is willing to listen and not be judgmental.
- *Loyal.* Stands beside his friend no matter what. Is someone you can always count on.
- *Trustworthy.* Is always honest, can keep a secret, doesn't lie or spread rumors.
- *Fun.* Has a good sense of humor and is fun to be with.

Three Keys to Making Friends

1. Smiles brighten the day for those who give and receive them.
2. Asking gets conversations started and lets the other person know you're interested in him.
3. Listening helps you learn about and know someone and show her that you care.[17]

ADDITIONAL SELF-ESTEEM BUILDERS

"Steer Them into Areas of Affirmation

Many sports don't emphasize size. Soccer, swimming, cross-country running, tennis, and gymnastics actually favor smaller competitors and have gained national prominence and popularity. There's more to life than football. Parents can find creative alternatives. Most high schools provide a smorgasbord of extracurricular activities, many of which provide excellent training for the future."[18] Children will always gravitate toward people, places, and things that make them feel good about themselves. Therefore, it's very important that we provide positive activities for them.

Parents accomplish this simply by noting a child's area of interest, then providing whatever help necessary for him to develop a measure of proficiency in that particular area. For example, provide tennis lessons or help a child complete the necessary steps to earn a scout badge.

Require a child to pick at least one extracurricular activity each school year.

A child who seemingly has no outside interests can be a challenge. However, a parent can help simply by identifying the uniqueness of that child. Help her recognize special interests, skills, and strengths. These can become a talent or a hobby that provides a refuge in the storm for an adolescent. Teach him to compensate for weaknesses and never to compare those areas with someone else's strengths. Affirm your child whenever possible and always praise effort.

Activities Kids Might Choose	
Bowling	Hockey
Girl Scouts	Karate
Boy Scouts	Boys Club
Piano	Band
Dance	Chorus
Little League	Service clubs
Skating	Drama clubs
Gymnastics	Big Brothers
Soccer	Big Sisters
Youth groups	YMCA programs
Swimming	School newspaper
Tennis	Jobs after school

Help Them Recognize Their Strengths and Skills

Kids are notorious for seeing only their weaknesses and then comparing those areas with everyone else's strengths. Remind kids that everyone has both.

Help children identify and become accustomed to talking about their strengths. In her book *How to Give Your Child a Great Self-Image*, Dr. Debora Phillips suggests that parents ask the following:

> Tell me something you like about yourself.
> *If the child has a difficult time answering the question try,*
> Tell me something you like about yourself today.
> Tell me something you felt good about today.
> Tell me something you did well today.
> Tell me something you enjoyed today.
> *Then listen with focused attention and respond with comments like*
> Really?
> No kidding?
> That's interesting, tell me more![19]

Encourage kids to compensate for their weak areas by focusing on their strengths.

Praise Often

Dr. Peter Favaro recommends that parents try to make sure that the positive things they say to a child outnumber the negative things by three to one.[20]

Look for ways to praise a child's skills, talents, and abilities. Many times this involves taking the time to identify areas where parents can compliment a child. Kids do neat things all the time, but because parents become accustomed to those things, they no longer compliment their children. For example, when a child has kitchen duty and has done the job well, many parents say nothing. Unfortunately, the child will hear a comment only if the job has been done poorly.

Likewise, when you compliment a child, be specific and concrete. For example: "You did a great job of cleaning your room. I especially like the way you made your bed and arranged your stuffed animals."

Finally, always praise your child for being what she is, not just for what she can do.

Wise Words

Mark Twain once said, "I can live two months on one good compliment!"

Encourage Often

Praise celebrates the results of a child's action. Encouragement celebrates a child's effort—regardless of the outcome. Always be sure to praise effort as well as accomplishment. Children will be more willing to take positive risks and try something new if they feel they don't have to be the best at it.

Comment on the process or feelings and thoughts that went into the work. Children glow when parents are interested in what goes on inside them as they produce. For example, you might note the strong strokes and warmth of the red coloring in your child's picture. Or acknowledge an attempt made by him to make you feel better.

I love the story about a mother who was sick in bed with the flu. Her darling daughter wanted so much to be a good nurse. She fluffed the pillows and brought a magazine for her mother to read. And then she even showed up with a surprise cup of tea.

"Why, you're such a sweetheart," the mother said as she drank her tea. "I didn't know you even know how to make tea."

"Oh yes," the little girl replied. "I learned by watching you. I put the tea leaves in a pan and then I put in the water, and I boiled it, and then I strained it into a cup. But I couldn't find the strainer, so I used the fly swatter instead."

"You what?" the mother screamed.

And the little girl said, "Oh, don't worry, Mom, I didn't use the new flyswatter, I used the old one."[21]

Moral of the story? Always encourage effort, even if you end up drinking some funny-tasting tea.

Encourage Positive Self-Talk

Your thoughts make up your attitudes about yourself. If they're negative, you probably feel pretty bad about yourself. On the other hand, if they're positive, you're probably feeling pretty good. Author Pat Palmer states that negative thoughts are a collection of bad habits, like biting your nails or popping your gum. He also suggests you can change this negative habit by following these simple steps:

- Decide to make a change.
- Pay attention to your thoughts.
- Make a commitment to do something about them.

For example, when you hear a negative thought, say *Stop!* Deliberately yell (inside your head), *Stop!* Then replace that negative thought with a positive one.[22]

Parents can be good role models by not putting themselves down with negative self-talk. Role-play making positive self-statements about yourself and others. Also, discuss other ways to use positive self-statements, such as problem solving and coping with stressful situ-ations.

Impact

If you think positive self-talk doesn't have an impact, when was the last time you programmed your VCR without saying, "I'm a smart person; I can do this!"

"Remind Them of Your Love and Acceptance"

"It's not too cool for teens to admit that they enjoy their parents' affirmation and affection, but we must not stop offering it. Teens long for acceptance from their parents. Your words and actions will often make the difference in their lives."[23] Tell children often that they're loved and are important to you!

Coping with the Four Bs

- Don't be surprised.
- Don't condemn.
- Understand the problem.
- Feel their hurt.
- Help where you can with clothing, hygiene, grooming, personal habits, and basic social skills.
- Steer them into areas of affirmation.
- Praise often.
- Encourage often.
- Remind them of your love and acceptance.

Additional Self-Esteem Builders

Author Fritz Ridenour offers several excellent ideas for building self-esteem. Slowly we incorporated them into our everyday lives with Heather.

Ridenour's first suggestion is "Decide on some specific things you'll concentrate on this month and the coming months to build your teenager's self-esteem."[24] By narrowing our focus, we identified one important aspect of Heather's self-esteem we felt needed immediate attention, and we started to work on it.

We concentrated our efforts on helping Heather feel more competent. When a child feels competent, she takes a can-do attitude. Feelings of competence, however, are based and built on successes. With Heather, we looked for anything that could be considered a success. Many times these were mini-successes or even partial successes, but for our purposes they still counted. And once counted, we then would offer praise, appreciation, acknowledgment, and encouragement. An excellent tool to use when doing this is home economist Barbara Gregg's list "100 Ways for Parents to Show Appreciation."[25]

100 Ways for Parents to Show Appreciation

1. You're on the right track now!
2. You're very good at that.
3. That is the best you've ever done.
4. I'm happy to see you working like that.
5. Nice try!
6. That's the way to do it.
7. I knew you could do it.
8. Now you've figured it out.
9. Now you have it.
10. Outstanding.
11. Keep working at it. You're getting better.
12. You're working hard today.
13. You're a great help!
14. You're getting better every day.
15. You're really growing up!
16. You figured that out fast.
17. You're a real prince (or princess).
18. You did that very well.
19. Nice going!
20. That was a kind thing you did.
21. Keep it up!
22. Super!
23. You make it look easy.
24. When I'm with you, I feel like singing.
25. I sure am happy you're my child.
26. That's my boy (or girl)!
27. I'm very proud of you.
28. I'm proud of the way you worked today.
29. You can do it!
30. You'll do better next time!
31. I think you've got it now.
32. Keep trying!
33. You've got it down pat!
34. Good thinking!
35. You've just about got it.
36. You're doing that much better today.
37. You're really going to town!
38. You're really improving.
39. I love you!
40. Superb!
41. That's much better!
42. That's really nice.
43. I like that.
44. Fantastic!
45. That's right.
46. You must have been practicing!
47. I appreciate your help.
48. One more time and you'll have it.
49. Sensational!
50. Nobody's perfect.
51. You certainly did well today.
52. You're doing beautifully.
53. Congratulations!
54. That is quite an improvement.
55. That's a masterpiece.
56. Excellent!
57. That's the best ever.
58. You're doing fine.
59. You're learning fast.
60. That's it!
61. Couldn't have done better myself.
62. You really make being a parent fun.
63. Terrific!
64. You did it that time!
65. You haven't missed a thing.
66. Now you've figured it out.
67. That's the way!
68. Dynamite!
69. Keep up the hard work.
70. Nothing can stop you now!
71. Good for you!
72. You've got your brain in gear today.
73. Wonderful!
74. You did a lot of work today!
75. Nice going.
76. Now that's what I call a fine job!
77. It's a pleasure to be a mommy (or daddy) when you work like that.

78. You've just about mastered that!
79. Right on!
80. Good remembering!
81. You're really learning a lot.
82. You've got a great future!
83. Fine!
84. You're doing the best.
85. Tremendous!
86. You outdid yourself today!
87. Perfect!
88. You remembered.
89. Now you have the hang of it.
90. Great!
91. Well, look at you go!
92. That gives me a happy feeling.
93. That's a friendly thing to do!
94. Clever!
95. You're like a beautiful (name object), (child's name).
96. Way to go.
97. Marvelous!
98. You're beautiful.
99. Congratulations! You got (name the behavior) right.
100. Lovely!

Another of Ridenour's suggestions that we used was "Be patient with their impatience, their tendency to label you as old-fashioned, out-of-date, ancient. It's amazing how modern you'll become in a few years if you last."[26]

Heather was always quite annoyed that I was so old-fashioned. All the other girls were doing the very things she wasn't allowed to do, or so she thought. Often she would scream, "You're single-handedly trying to destroy my social life!" and "Lighten up and get with the times!" However, I hung in there. Interestingly, as Heather grew older, she became very protective of her little sister. Often I heard Heather say, "Mom, you're not going to let her do that, are you?"

Our patience through the years with Heather's impatience really paid off.

A parent's best bet?

1. Understand the physical and emotional changes that occur during adolescence.

2. "Feeling part of the group" is important. Help where you can with clothing, grooming, hygiene, and personal habits.

3. Teach and reinforce basic social skills.

4. Steer your child into areas of affirmation and help him recognize his strengths and skills.

5. Be your child's cheerleader by offering plenty of praise and encouragement.

6. Memorize and use the list of 100 ways to show your child appreciation.

Chapter Seven

■ ■ ■

SAVED BY THE BELL

Making school a positive experience

School is a training ground for children, with the primary goal of preparing them for life as adults. Unfortunately, kids can perceive school as an "end" rather than a "means to an end." They fail to understand that class work teaches them to reason, analyze, and conceptualize. And these skills help them, as adults, to find ways to effectively handle problems at their jobs, with their families, and in their relationships.

Several years ago, the ABC special "American Kids: Teaching Them to Think" noted that the average factory jobs in the new millennium will require at least thirteen years of education. Instead of strong backs, employers will look for sharp minds as the demand for workers with computing, reasoning, and problem-solving skills continually increases. The uneducated adults of tomorrow will be unable to compete in the workplace and will be ill-equipped to handle the complexities of the twenty-first century.

What does this mean for your children? It's important that they make the most of their time in school, and that you help them learn and prepare for the future.

THE VALUE OF LEARNING

Because parents serve as a window to the world for their children, your values and attitudes easily rub off on your kids. This is especially true with younger children. If, for example, you think poorly of a teacher or believe that education is a waste of time, your kids probably will, too.

Former U.S. Secretary of Education Richard W. Riley states,

> The American family is the rock on which a solid education can be built. I have seen examples all over this nation where two-parent families, single parents, stepparents, grandparents, aunts, and uncles are providing strong family support for their children to learn. If families teach the love for learning, it can make all the difference in the world.[1]

In light of this statement, it's vital for you to maintain a positive attitude when talking to your children about school, and to continually stress the importance of an education. Starting when they're in preschool, you can encourage children to value learning. As they grow older, you can reinforce the idea that dropping out of school isn't an option for them.

Help children establish clear goals and see an education as a way to achieve those goals. Also help them see that an education can enable them to realize a productive, exciting future of untold possibilities.

How Parents Can Help

Parents first help children in school by taking an interest in their education. At home, take the time to instill basic values and provide plenty of love and discipline. Set appropriate guidelines not only concerning behavior in the classroom but for assignments as well. High school principal Robert Williams suggests that parents teach children the basic values of right and wrong, the importance of commitment, hard work, sacrifice, and respect for authority.

Read daily to younger children and help them develop a love for books. Provide positive reading material by subscribing to fun, educational magazines and a daily newspaper. Let them see you read. Also, acquaint kids with the public library and encourage them to get library cards. Establish a family library day once a week or once per check-out period. Encourage kids to read to you, and then talk about the books.

Be a positive role model. Become an active learner by seeking out information. Enroll in a class at a local college or through an adult education program at a high school. Read and study together. Make learning a family affair!

When Parents Get Involved, Their Children . . .

- Get better grades and test scores.
- Graduate from high school at higher rates.
- Are more likely to go on to higher education.
- Are better behaved and have more positive attitudes.[2]

Schedule homework into your child's life. Just as your child may have soccer practice at 4:00 P.M., she needs a set time each day for homework. This ends discussions about when it will be done and puts a halt to the child's stalling tactics. Talk to her about homework assignments; ask questions about it, and see whether it's completed. Help her manage the workload by dividing it into small doses to eliminate needing to complete a two-week science project in one night.

If possible, provide a family computer or access to a computer. Computer skills are crucial for future jobs. Help your child learn early how to type and to work software.

Limit TV viewing. Studies show that academic achievement drops sharply for children who watch more than ten hours of TV during the school week.

Never take anything for granted and continually check your child's school progress. Just because you haven't heard from the school doesn't automatically mean all is well with the child. Obtain information from both the school and the child at arbitration. Also, determine the number of academic credits needed in each subject required for graduation, and continually be aware of your high school student's status.

Start a school file for each child and find a safe place for it. Develop the habit of carefully reading everything you receive from school. In each child's file keep all relevant school correspondence as well as standardized test results and report cards. This is an excellent place to keep deadlines and requirements for scholarships, loan applications, and admission applications for college-bound students.

Attend school orientations and meet teachers, noting their names, the subjects they teach, and the class periods they teach your children. Also get information about the best time to contact them concerning school-related matters. Again, all this information should be kept in the children's school files for quick reference.

Tell the teachers, counselors, and school administrators that you're interested in your children's academic progress and request that they notify you immediately of any problems. However, don't hesitate to contact the teacher if you have a concern.

Strong evidence suggests that the more parents become involved in their children's education, the better those children do in school. Teachers are much more likely to take an interest in a child when they know the parents. By getting involved, parents can make sure a child doesn't become just a name on a roster. Get to know the names of your children's teachers, principals, and counselors, and develop a good relationship with each. Consider becoming a room parent or a chaperone for field trips.

Finally, attend school-related activities such as band concerts, athletic events, and awards programs. Celebrate a child's accomplishments big and small. Whether he's the star quarterback or spends most of the time on the bench; whether she wins the spelling bee or makes it through only half of the cuts; celebrate your child's success and reinforce his participation.

PROBLEMS AT SCHOOL

When kids do have problems in school, they usually can be categorized into four major areas: discipline, academics, social acceptance, and home environment.

Discipline

If a child can't exercise self-control, he's going to have a difficult time in the classroom. Usually (but not always) a child who has a discipline problem in school has received little or no consistent discipline at home. Therefore, it's vital for parents to understand the importance of instilling discipline, values, and standards for conduct early in a child's life. Failing in this will only handicap the child as he struggles with self-control and appropriate conduct in the classroom.

In some cases, however, the child might not be able to control his behavior. Children who are emotionally handicapped—that is, afflicted with hyperactivity, attention deficit disorder (ADD), or attention deficit disorder with hyperactivity (ADHD)—can experience behavioral problems.

Misbehavior in the classroom might also be the result of alcohol or drug abuse on the part of the teenager. The number-one drug problem among teenagers today is alcohol abuse, and a great deal of drinking is done on junior and senior high school campuses.

Possible Solutions

1. Understand that the responsibility for instilling discipline, values, and standards is the parents' and not the school's. Start early in teaching children self-control and appropriate classroom behavior.
2. Set boundaries that include behavior in school. This might mean weekly progress

reports or even daily behavior progress reports for younger children. Be sure to reward the behavior you want repeated!

3. Consider enrolling your child in an athletic program that stresses discipline and self-control, such as karate or tae kwon do.

4. If the behavioral problem has been ongoing, request that the child be tested to determine if there is an emotional handicap, hyperactivity, or another disorder. If a problem is diagnosed, immediately address the needs of that child with the school psychologist. Medication and therapy might be necessary.

5. Request a teacher that can work well with your child. As a rule, most administrations prefer parents not ask for a specific teacher by name. However, you can describe your child's traits (is sensitive, hyperactive, easily distracted) and describe what you want from a teacher (someone who is warm and nurturing and provides classroom structure, routines). Always put your request in writing and have it put in your child's file.

6. If a teen has an alcohol or drug abuse problem, seek immediate treatment. Getting stoned or wasted should never be tolerated—anywhere!

7. Any time a child is chronically angry, full of rage, and acting out, consider individual or family therapy. The inappropriate behavior might be a symptom of a much bigger underlying problem.

Academics

Because kids rarely want to admit that they have trouble learning in general or in a particular subject, acting out becomes a safe alternative. It's very important to young people that others don't perceive them as slow or not very bright.

In fact, a child who is failing school might be very bright but hampered by something else. She might not know how to study effectively for a test or might lack the discipline to complete homework assignments.

Some might experience health problems resulting from poor diet or lack of sleep. Additionally, a child can suffer hearing or vision loss or even dyslexia and not be aware of it. The child who seemingly won't learn perhaps is one who simply can't learn.

Finally, a child might not be interested in school. Or he might simply be bored with the classes he's taking and is underchallenged.

To Work or Not to Work?

High school students with jobs do poorer in school, miss class more often, and spend less time on homework than those who don't work. The effect is most serious among teens who work more than fifteen to twenty hours a week. More than two-thirds of all high school juniors and seniors are employed.[3]

Sixteen-year-old Brad was falling further and further behind at school. He couldn't stay focused and slept through most of his morning classes. Often he would skip school. After his mom met with the school guidance counselor, they determined that Brad was of above-average intelligence and capable of doing well in school. But he also was working twenty-two hours a week busing dishes. By the time he got home from work, he was too tired for homework. And when he went to school, he couldn't concentrate. Because the average teen needs between seven and nine hours of sleep a night, Brad was physically exhausted. He and his mom decided he should quit working, but agreed that once he obtained Cs or better, he could work on weekends.

Possible Solutions

1. If a child is chronically failing, request that she be tested to determine if there is a learning disability. Ask the school psychologist to help assess the test results and aid in determining the best course of action. If there is a learning disability, consider private tutoring with a learning problem specialist. Also consider an alternative educational program that specializes in small classes and individual attention.

2. Make sure the child is in good physical health. An exam with your family doctor might be necessary. Have his vision and hearing checked. If glasses are needed, make sure he likes the frames and is comfortable with the way they make him look. Most teenagers would rather not see and fail than wear glasses they don't like.

3. Assess the child's diet. Teen years are a time for very rapid growth that requires better nutrition than hamburgers and potato chips. Also, because of rapid growth, a teen may have difficulty functioning on six or seven hours of sleep at night. Make sure she gets plenty of rest.

4. If the child is bored, determine why. Seek help in directing him toward more intellectually challenging classes.

   However, if he's bored because he's just not interested in school, consider alternative education programs. For example, during a teen's junior and senior years, many schools offer programs that allow students to go to school half the day and work the other half.

Social Acceptance

Often social problems can be more troublesome to correct than academic problems. A child who suffers from poor self-esteem often will suffer socially at school. "Low self-esteem is the single most powerful root cause of America's steadily increasing public school dropout rate," states Professor Hayman Kite.[4]

According to Tammy Austin, senior program manager for Foster Care Services, "Especially at risk are second-semester sixth-grade students. The transition between elementary and middle school is very difficult for some children, and they get lost in the peer-pecking order."

Kids who don't fit in socially will often go to any lengths to do so. Unfortunately, because of their incessant need to belong, many adolescents will become involved with any peer group that takes them. They also might turn to alcohol or drug abuse or sex as they struggle for peer attention and acceptance. Or they might simply withdraw or develop a negative outlook about school or a defensive attitude toward those around them.

Also, truancy becomes an option for some teens who feel frightened and intimidated because they're being physically threatened. Unfortunately, 20 percent of all schoolchildren are repeat victims of bullies.[5]

Relationship problems with a boyfriend or girlfriend can cause a teen to take a nosedive at school. Because these relationships tend to be intense, they can become all-consuming. Fortunately, most are short-lived.

Finally, a teen could be influenced by a peer group that has already dropped out of school. Algebra can be tough to tackle if you know your best friend is tackling the beach or even a job to pay for his new Camaro.

Possible Solutions

1. Understand the importance of a child's feelings and her need to belong. Parents should do whatever is necessary to help a child feel better about herself. This might include helping with her clothing or grooming. Also, basic social skills are not necessarily innate qualities: a crash course on making friends or how to be a friend might be very beneficial. Additionally, some specific behaviors might alienate her from other children. For example, is she loud or obnoxious?

2. Provide opportunities for positive peer group interaction apart from school, such as special hobby clubs, organized sports, or church youth group activities. Contact the school guidance counselor if your child is being teased or ridiculed. Peer counseling or a mentor program might be made available. If a child is being threatened, make an appointment with the school guidance counselor and principal and insist that the problem be addressed. Put this request in writing and ask that it be included in your child's file at school.

3. Take your child's romantic relationships seriously; be available, listen, and care.

4. In as subtle a way as possible, limit the amount of time your child spends with friends who have dropped out of school.

What to Do If Your Child Is Being Bullied

- Acknowledge his feelings.
- Role-play appropriate responses.
- Determine if there is an area where you can help him fit in.
- Provide opportunities for positive peer group interaction apart from school.
- If the problem persists, alert the appropriate school official and insist he or she takes action.

Home Environment

Every family has its own set of problems. Some simply have to do with the way we live our lives. Many experts agree that the most important elements in children's lives include regular routines, domestic rituals, consistency, and a sense that their parents know and care about them. Yet often these are the very things that get jettisoned with hurried lives and frazzled parents.

Unfortunately, even more-serious problems might include such things as poor relationships between family members, unemployment, divorce, poverty, and alcohol or drug addiction of family members. Problems, even serious family problems, don't always have to be detrimental. However, these types of difficulties become destructive if children see their parents collapsing under the weight of their problems.

Although a bright kid, nine-year-old Eric was having difficulty across the board. Because Eric's parents refurbished older homes by moving in, fixing them up, selling them, and moving on, Eric had already been enrolled in four different schools. Additionally, his home life was chaotic because of his father's serious drinking problem and the construction site environment in which he lived.

After being alerted to the problem by the school guidance counselor, Eric's mom got busy. Although her husband would not go to Alcoholics Anonymous, she became active in

Al-Anon (a support group for families of alcoholics), and Eric saw a therapist at school. Additionally, she refused to move again, volunteered in Eric's classroom, and provided him with some stability at home. This allowed him to stay focused, make friends, and become involved in sports at school.

Possible Solutions

1. Watching parents constructively deal with major problems can actually benefit children. It provides them with the opportunity to learn important concepts such as problem solving, decision making, stress management, and goal setting. Often we would tell Heather when she was having a problem, "There isn't a problem in having a problem. The problem is in not doing something about it. Every problem has a solution. We just have to find it!"

2. Cut down on the chaos at home—where's my shoe, my book bag, . . . Instead, establish consistent rules and routines. Explain what you want and refuse to argue. Stick with it, even if bending the rules might be easier at times. Consistency pays off in the end.

3. Finding the best solution to the problem might involve tapping resources outside the family, such as professional counseling. By doing this, you teach children one place to go for help.

ADDRESSING BIGGER SCHOOL TROUBLES

1. If the child's behavioral problem has been ongoing, ask to review his school file. Parents legally have the right to see their children's records. Ask the school psychologist or guidance counselor to review the records with you. This will enable you to better understand the various test scores, teacher assessments, and behavioral labels such as ADD or ADHD.

2. At the beginning of each school year, make sure *you* fill out all information cards requested by your child's school. This will eliminate the possibility that his records contain incorrect information or false signatures. Some teens will list their personal phone number as the number to call to report school absences and will sign their parents' names. Then they can receive important phone calls from school and sign their parents' names on progress reports and other documents.

3. A parent can have a child's school records flagged so that if she's absent from school, a counselor from the guidance department will notify the parent instead of the parent being notified by a recorded message.

If truancy is a problem, determine why the child is skipping school and address that problem area. Establish a rule concerning skipping school with an appropriate consequence. For example: "You may not skip school. To do so will result in either Mom or Dad going to school with you the very next school day." The parent can take a folding chair, a Thermos of coffee, and a very good book and escort the child from class to class. (Always check with the school administration prior to doing this.)

4. Before a suspension occurs, request that the child be given only in-school suspensions. Instead of a three-day holiday at home, she then will be required to spend three days at school on suspension.

5. Request weekly progress reports for all the child's classes. At arbitration, establish a rule that includes a required weekly grade point average in each class and a consequence for not having it.

CONFERENCES

When a problem arises at school that requires a teacher conference, first address the problem at length with the child at arbitration. Carefully explain the problem as it has been presented to you and ask the child the following questions. Take detailed notes about his answers. If the child won't respond, list these questions and ask him to answer them in writing.

Questions About Problems at School

- What is the problem as you see it?
- How long has the problem been going on?
- How well do you get along with this teacher? Do you have the same problems with other teachers?
- Do you understand the subject material?
- Do you participate in class?
- How would you describe your behavior in class?
- How well do you get along with the kids in this class?
- What kind of solution do you see to the problem?

Once you have a clear understanding of the problem from the child's perspective, make an appointment for a parent-child-teacher conference. A positive parental attitude when dealing with the school administration or individual teachers is important. When addressing specific problems, be cooperative rather than defensive, and don't try to place blame. Implement a win-win approach with a statement such as "How can I help you help my child in this area?" Ideally, this will enable everyone to work together to help the child.

At the parent-child-teacher conference, ask the teacher basically the same questions you asked the child. Again, take detailed notes. Compare answers, examine the facts, and identify a specific problem or problem areas. Then brainstorm all solutions to the problem. Again, make sure your attitude is nonthreatening and is one of helping the teacher help the child.

If you strike out completely with a teacher and are totally dissatisfied, there are additional steps that can be taken. However, make sure the problem is serious enough to warrant going further.

1. Consult with the principal. Using your conference notes, present the facts to the principal and ask him or her to mediate. Again, be sure to take notes of the meeting for future reference.
2. Go to the school board. Again using notes you took at the teacher's conference and your meeting with the principal, present the facts to the school board and ask them to mediate.
3. Look for alternative educational programs. They may be the only solution when a child is having extreme difficulty, is at risk of dropping out, or has already dropped out of school.
4. Finally, remember that all teachers and guidance counselors are not the same. As in all careers, some people perform better than others. A good math teacher can mean all the difference in the world for a child struggling with the basics. And a good guidance counselor can help teens and parents assess test scores and detect and correct problem areas. Always be on the lookout for teachers or guidance counselors that can best help your kids. Before school starts, request those people.

A parent's best bet?

1. Teach the love of learning. Express excitement and interest in the different subjects your child is learning. Emphasize the importance of your child's education and its application to the real world.

2. Maintain a positive attitude about your children's principal, teachers, and counselors, and develop a good relationship with each.

3. Take an active interest in your child's education. Attend school orientation, activities, and other school-related functions.

4. At the beginning of each school year, request from the school a calendar of important dates. Add to your master calendar all relevant school dates such as orientations, open houses, and holidays.

5. Establish a school file for each child in the family. Develop a habit of reading all the materials from school and filing important information.

6. Celebrate accomplishments both big and small!

Chapter Eight

■ ■ ■

HOW CAN I LOVE YOU?

I'm not sure I even like you

Loving a child when you're not sure you like him is very much like a high-wire act. It calls for some extraordinary balancing and excellent concentration, and it can prove to be exceedingly difficult. Loving a child you may not like calls for basic unconditional love. Above all else, unconditional love provides the cornerstone for the emotional well-being of a child.

Surprisingly, you start with loving yourself unconditionally. To have an impact on children today, especially those who are troubled, parents need to be at their very best.

Perhaps I can clarify this best with the analogy of the lifeguard and the swimming pool. Imagine sending your child, who is a poor swimmer, to a pool with all his friends for an afternoon of fun and frolic. Being a good parent, you would call to ask about the lifeguard. How frustrating it would be if your conversation went something like this:

> "My son doesn't swim very well and wants to spend the afternoon at the pool with his friends. Please tell me about the lifeguard who will be on duty."
>
> "Certainly! This particular lifeguard is very well liked by all the kids who swim here."
>
> "Wonderful!" you might reply, "But how well does he swim?"
>
> "Well, he's really dedicated to saving kids. In addition to that, he's an excellent student and involved in many extracurricular activities. He really is the type of kid who would make any mother proud."
>
> Again, you might reply, "Great! But can he swim?"
>
> "No, as a matter of fact, he can't swim. But he sure is a real nice guy!"

Would you still let your child go? Probably not. Instead you'd ask, "How in the world can this lifeguard be expected to save anyone if he can't even save himself?" His intentions may be very honorable, but to be effective at his job, he has to be strong and capable in the water.

Families are like that. Good intentions are great, but to deal with children effectively, parents need to be strong and capable. Fear, worry, and resentment are difficult to govern, and anger is almost impossible to control if a parent is physically and mentally exhausted. Like the lifeguard, a parent can help others only when he can save himself.

Start by taking responsibility for taking care of yourself. Putting a premium on yourself by treating yourself with dignity has an interesting effect: it forces others to do so as well.

Too often parents put "doormat" signs on their foreheads and let their rights, needs, and desires be trampled upon. Too often they allow their own identities to become tightly wrapped up with their children's. They feel that only by sacrificing their own lives can they win their children's good behavior, sympathy, and love. Sadly, the only thing accomplished is that the parents become martyrs and are neither appreciated nor respected by anyone—especially their children.

This is exactly what took place in my home. Heather had two standards of conduct: one for our home and one for everywhere else. I discovered this only after continually hearing from neighbors and friends how wonderful and well behaved Heather was. My Heather? The one with the four-letter-word vocabulary and howitzer mouth?

Then I realized that of course she was wonderful—there! Heather knew that if she pulled the stuff next door that she was pulling at home, she would promptly be shown the door with instructions never to return. Other folks liked themselves far too much to put up with any verbal bashing from my teenager.

What lesson did I learn? Only when you treat yourself well will others treat you accordingly. Then and there I took "doormat" off my forehead and learned how to take better care of myself.

For years I had a difficult time dealing with stress, anger, and resentment. I kept things bottled up until I exploded and acted in totally inappropriate ways. Because stress is cumulative, it soon took very little to trigger my temper. And at times I acted like a complete fool. Then, of course, I felt guilty about what I'd done, which only added to my stress, and so it went. For example, once when Heather and I were grocery shopping, we had a terrible argument and caused quite a scene. To this day I can't remember exactly what we fought about. However, what happened during the argument is very clear. The memory of that day is imprinted on my brain forever.

Heather had become an expert at punching my buttons. She did so that day with her usual flair. Only this time I didn't think through the problem so I could respond with a cool head. Instead, I reacted very badly. In the bakery section, I bashed, belted, clobbered, and walloped Heather with a loaf of Wonder Bread. As my anger subsided, breadcrumbs lay on the floor and bread dust fell from the air. With tears in my eyes and bread in my hair, I stood in horror and gasped at the substantial crowd that had gathered. Heather stood there covered with bread, looking innocent and sweet. She smiled and said, "Well, I guess I should be glad we weren't in the canned goods aisle."

Yes, I was a real candidate for some remedial work on taking better care of myself.

According to Patricia Jakubowski in her book *The Assertive Option*, parents have some very basic assertive rights:

1. Act in ways that promote dignity and self-respect as long as others' rights are not violated.
2. Be treated with respect.
3. Say no and not feel guilty.
4. Experience and express your feelings.
5. Take time to slow down and think.
6. Change your mind.
7. Ask for what you want.

8. Do less than you're humanly capable of doing.
9. Ask for information.
10. Make mistakes.
11. Feel good about yourself.[1]

STRESS MANAGEMENT

Because stress was a real problem for me, learning how to cope more effectively with it became a priority in my life. Psychologist Penny Lukin makes several excellent points on stress management. She states, however, that first it's important to recognize the signs of *distress,* or ineffective coping: giving up and becoming depressed; experiencing an inability to concentrate; becoming argumentative, irritable, anxious; or developing stress-related illnesses such as heart palpitations, insomnia, headaches, high blood pressure, neck and back pain, ulcers, or stomachaches. Walloping Heather with a loaf of bread was a definite sign of ineffective coping!

Also important, Dr. Lukin notes, is to eliminate the threat of stress by putting yourself in control and finding appropriate ways to manage your stress. She suggests the following:

Lower expectations of yourself and others. Becoming more realistic with your expectations is both freeing and empowering. Only when Heather and I were freed from my unrealistic expectations of being the perfect mother of a perfect daughter could we become all that we could be!

Be optimistic. Abraham Lincoln once said, "People generally are as happy or as miserable as they make up their minds to be." How very true. Recently Harry, a widower with three teenagers, reminded a PWOP class how very true this is. Within two years, his wife died of cancer, he experienced financial hardship, and the kids were acting out. Still he had a smile on his face, laughter in his eyes, and an outlook that said, "I have hope for my family and we are going to be fine." Remember to think positively! People who say, "I can," and people who say, "I can't," are both right.

Signs of Stress

- You're easily upset by things you have no control over, such as a traffic jam.
- You feel rushed and impatient, finishing other people's sentences and talking quickly.
- Your neck muscles are tight and feel stiff when you move your head from side to side.
- You find yourself clenching your jaw muscles.
- You feel burned out or tired all the time.[2]

Take a stress break. A stress break is any activity that gives you a new perspective and reduces your stress. This can include going to the movies, watching TV, reading a good book or magazine, fishing, sewing, talking to a friend, taking time for a hobby, or—on a larger scale—a camping trip or mini-vacation. What will work for one will not work for another The important thing is to find what works for you!

Work off tension through physical exercise. A good physical workout not only relieves tension but also improves your stamina and produces a sense of confidence and well-being. This might include jogging, swimming, walking, biking, tennis, gardening, or working out.

One of the first things I did in my stress management program was to join a health spa. When I felt the stress build, I worked out instead of allowing it to accumulate and possibly explode. For example, one evening Heather and I had a terrible argument. However, rather than reacting and dumping my frustration and anger on Heather, I went to work out. Terribly distraught, I found myself at the spa, riding a LifeCycle on level five (the most difficult level) as I wept into a towel. I still chuckle whenever I remember hearing one young attendant saying to the other that night, "I know it's time to close, but I'm not going to tell her she has to get off the bike!" For years, working out helped me keep my sanity and my stress under control. The bonus, of course, was that I also felt great.

Avoid self-medications such as drugs or alcohol. Alcohol and drugs such as tranquilizers are depressants that will depress you and your system!

Eat a balanced diet. Nutritionist Pam Smith states, "A stressed-out person's blood sugar may fluctuate wildly, causing mood swings, irritability, fatigue, and food cravings." Unfortunately, the food we crave the most (usually something chocolate!) during times of stress is not what our bodies need. Ms. Smith suggests we include complex carbohydrates in our diets for energy, avoid fats and sugar, eat lightly and more often, drink plenty of water, and cut back on stimulants such as caffeine and nicotine.[3]

HUMOR HELPS

Raising teenagers is serious business, but you may be taking yourself a little too seriously. While taking Heather very seriously, I learned to keep things in perspective and not to take myself all that seriously. Everything didn't really have to be a matter of life or death. Besides, Heather took herself seriously enough for both of us.

Realizing that Heather's conduct wasn't directed at me helped me. Here was a kid who at times was out of control, but her behavior wasn't directed at me. Granted, I often caught the fallout, but that was all it was.

Mary G. Durkin, in her book *Making Your Family Work,* suggests that you can lighten your burden—and make the task of parenting more rewarding—if you learn to laugh: "When you trip, humor will soften the fall. You can then approach seemingly unsolvable family problems with the old cliché, 'If I don't laugh, I'll cry.'"[4] Psychiatrist Christian Hageseth describes a sense of humor as a broad, optimistic perception of life, and suggests that it can ease tension and improve communication.[5]

By keeping my sense of humor and lightening up a little, I learned that Heather and I could actually have a little fun. It's important to remember, however, never to confuse humor and ridicule. Laugh *with* your children, never *at* them. And teach all the family members that a good time should never be at the expense of one person in the family.

TIME MANAGEMENT

Manage your time and energy wisely. Learn to establish goals and set priorities. Simplify your life as much as possible. Be realistic about what's important and needs to be done today, and then make a list of those things. Believe it or not, there are only twenty-four hours in a day. A sure way to burn out is to cram thirty-six hours of activity into twenty-four.

Instead, realistically allocate time to each item on your list of important things that need to be done. Always make sure you include time for yourself. If you find that you have too many things to do and not enough time, put the unfinished things first on your list of things for tomorrow. Does this mean at times you don't get everything done? Yes, it does.

But it also means you'll finish the race because you've conserved your energy by pacing yourself. Parents can avoid burning out only by avoiding emotional and physical overload.

Working Moms and Single Parents

For a long time women struggled with the myth that they could have it all and do it all. Weekly, we watched Clare Huxtable on *The Cosby Show* as she (without help) managed a successful law practice, maintained a beautiful home, and took wonderful care of the needs of her large family. She was never frazzled, she always looked great, and she never served TV dinners. How in the world did she do it? She didn't. Clare was a fictional character. There really aren't any supermoms.

In the real world, only with careful planning and a great deal of help from family members can working moms and single parents successfully juggle career and family. To do a better job of balancing home and career, consider incorporating the following suggestions into your family routine.

- Make a list of everything that needs to be accomplished at home in order for things to run smoothly. Be sure to include all household tasks such as cleaning, errands, yard work, grocery shopping, laundry, menu planning, meal preparation, and making lunches. Then, as much as possible, relax your standards and delegate these jobs to family members. Use the "Daily Stuff" section of your children's workbooks to assign these tasks. For example, rather than having a specific day to clean house, assign a house-cleaning chore daily.
- Make grocery shopping a family affair. For years my family made this a family outing. Our evening would start with an early dinner at a local cafeteria followed by our weekly grocery shopping. Because there were four of us, we usually could complete this task in less than thirty minutes.
- Park your grocery cart in a central place and divide your grocery list among family members. Even younger children are capable of getting the cereal and dog food. However, make sure everyone sticks to the list to avoid overspending. The added bonus, of course, is that you have plenty of help putting away the groceries!
- A major stressor for many working moms is meal planning. Plan weekly menus, thus eliminating morning decisions concerning dinner. Always double recipes and freeze half. Post an ongoing grocery list on the refrigerator and encourage all family members to add items to this list when they see the supply running low.
- Make food preparation easier by requiring teens or older family members to prepare an evening meal once a week. Younger children can assist by setting the table or making a salad. Assign a teen or older family member the task of making lunches for the next day.
- Assign a laundry day for each child and require him to be responsible for his laundry. Younger children who can't master the washer and dryer are great at folding things like washcloths and towels.
- Allow teens to "purchase" car time by running errands such as going to the cleaners or taking the dog to the vet.
- Finally, it's important for single parents and working moms to provide decompression time when the family comes home in the evening. Establish a coming-home ritual that includes either taking the telephone off the hook or leaving the answering machine on

for the first thirty minutes everyone is home. Provide a healthy snack to take the edge off hunger until dinner is served. Allow yourself twenty minutes of uninterrupted time to relax and unwind by taking a nap, walking around the block, or taking a leisurely bath.

One single mom recently shared the success she was experiencing balancing family and career. She had been on the verge of burnout because it had become easier to do things herself than to go through the hassle of getting her four kids to help. "For years," she exclaimed, "I felt in control of everything but my home life, which was in total chaos. However, by implementing the *Parenting Without Pressure* program, I now have a method to restore order and allow us to work as a team!"

Because weekdays were often hectic, she organized the upcoming week for the family on Sunday afternoons. After determining which household tasks needed to be accomplished, she assigned these to the kids by filling out the "Daily Stuff" section of their workbooks for the entire week. On a daily basis, she made additions and revisions and added personal notes. Everyone knew up front what was expected of him or her for the following week. And for the first time, Mom could count on the cooperation of her children.

Finding Resources Outside the Family

Find resources in the area that can help make your job as a parent easier. Surround yourself with a circle of friends whose advice and judgment you respect, folks you can count on to listen, to care, to understand.

For example, Elaine and Samantha had been friends for years. They attended the same church and they had a weekly tennis and lunch date. They were there for each other through the good times and the bad. When Samantha's son was charged with vehicular manslaughter, Elaine was there. She dried tears, brainstormed options, and simply acted as a sounding board.

Friends

A friend is a gift you give yourself. And talking out problems with a friend can reduce stress. It provides you with the opportunity to get things off your chest and helps put things in perspective.

Also, religious organizations offer great adult support groups and activities for young people. Organizations such as the Big Brother and Big Sister programs and Boy Scouts and Girl Scouts are excellent for kids. Many organizations and clubs will sponsor kids who need financial help to participate in sports programs. Most telephone directories have a Human Services listing of organizations and services for adults and young people. Find what is there for you. Consider it a fact-finding mission! Be creative and innovative.

Summers can be a nightmare for parents with school-age children left unattended at home. Because summer programs at the Boys Club and YMCA fill up rapidly, one mom starts calling in January for her children's placement. In June, when many parents are frantically looking for something their kids can do, this mom isn't stressed. Talk about great planning!

TAKING CARE OF SIGNIFICANT RELATIONSHIPS

Finally, in addition to being good to yourself, spend time focusing on and maintaining your marriage or significant relationship. Everything tends to get lost when dealing with children in crisis, especially relationships between the adults in the family. Unfortunately, marriage is a frequent casualty in such cases. Couples tend to concentrate all their available energy on the misbehaving child. That child can easily become the focal point of the family. Conversations, family outings, work schedules, and even needs of the other children in the family become secondary to the dysfunctional child.

What an impossible situation for the family and a terrible burden for the child! You may need professional help in learning how to shift your focus. Behavior patterns become habits, and habits are hard to break. This is one behavior pattern that is destructive and should be eliminated immediately.

When we realized this was happening in our own family, Herb and I set about changing it. It had been a very long time since we'd emotionally connected and talked about anything other than Heather. One of the neatest things my husband and I did during this time was to work on getting reacquainted. We learned to schedule date nights and make them a top priority. During those dates, our children and their problems were forbidden conversation topics. Instead, we worked on recreating or developing similar interests and activities apart from the children. One objective was more important, however. We worked at keeping a sense of fun, intimacy, and romance alive in our relationship.

One of our funniest moments occurred during this time. During dinner on one of our first date nights, I endearingly looked up at my husband and exclaimed, "My gosh, Herb, is that you? When did you lose your hair?"

Dates for You and Your Mate

- Picnic in your favorite park.
- Cook a special meal together.
- Catch your favorite movie.
- Watch the sunset.
- Discover new places.
- Go for a long walk.
- Go for a bike ride.
- Learn a new sport together.
- Meet for lunch.
- Schedule an at-home romance date.
- Plan a bed and breakfast date.
- Go to a community concert.[6]

The Thompsons, parents of a blended family of eight, got very creative with their weekly dating. Their weekends were filled with kids' activities, and weeknights were consumed with laundry, cleaning, grocery shopping, and catch-up. However, both Maddie and Jim scheduled a two-hour lunch on Tuesdays. They met at home, and because everyone was at school, they always added a little spice to the salad!

When couples make maintaining the marriage a priority, the results permeate the entire family. Not only does it make the family unit stronger and more capable of handling adversity, it puts that challenging child where he belongs—in the role of a child in the family.

Once you've accomplished these two things—taking care of yourself and taking care of your marriage or significant relationship—you've established a firm base from which you can show your children that all-important unconditional love.

A parent's best bet?

1. List those activities that help you unwind and relax. Commit yourself to doing one of these things daily for the next week.

2. List activites you're doing that aren't related to your job; for example, writing your neighborhood newsletter. Ask yourself, "Do I really need to be doing this?" If the answer is no, take it off your list.

3. Practice time management. Buy a daily calendar. Make a list (in order of priority) of those things that need to be done daily. Remember to include time for yourself. Practice working your way through the list, remembering that those things not accomplished are simply rolled over to the next day.

4. Establish a weekly afternoon or evening date with your spouse and observe it consistently.

5. Consider the following suggestions from Dave and Claudia Arp's book, 52 Dates for You and Your Mate.

Your Marriage

Treat the word *marriage* as a verb, not a noun. It's an ongoing process that requires time and attention.

Chapter Nine

■ ■ ■

LOVING UNCONDITIONALLY

Providing the cornerstone for emotional well-being

Conditional love is just that—love that is conditioned on something. A person who loves conditionally says, "I'll love you if you do something to make me proud." That something might be doing well in school or excelling at a sport. Often conditional love is accompanied by expectations that are almost impossible for a child to meet. How many times have you seen a boy trying to please his father by being the star quarterback, or heard a disheartened girl explain why she made 95 percent on an exam rather than 100 percent, or heard a discouraged teen say, "What's the use? There's no pleasing my parents anyway."

Tragically, this parenting pattern often produces kids who either spend a lifetime trying to please a parent or simply quit trying. And sadly, like most dysfunctional patterns, this one tends to repeat itself. The child becomes an angry and bitter adult who was unable to measure up as a young person and now sets unrealistic expectations for those around him.

A person who loves unconditionally says, "I love you no matter what—no matter what you look like, what you act like, what you happen to do, or where you happen to find yourself in life. My love for you is not based on your love for me or on anything else."

Because as parents we are but mere mortals, total unconditional love is impossible to obtain. But the closer you can come to it, the healthier your family will be. It takes a mature person to look at a little one with all her imperfections and convey to her that not only is she loved immensely, but also she's a person of immeasurable worth. Oh, for years I strived for such maturity with Heather!

LOVING THE LEPER

Putting emotional distance between you and your child's behavior is perhaps the most important thing you can do. More than anything else, this will enable you to consistently give your child unconditional love.

Kids who are emotionally and behaviorally out of control can go right for the jugular when dealing with loved ones. Many of these kids are capable of causing unbelievable emotional pain. Such kids commonly target one parent and become experts at knowing that parent's vulnerabilities. They then unrelentingly attack those areas, causing indescribable pain.

When this happens, hurt and angry parents tend to square off and verbally retaliate. Unfortunately, with this kind of response, some parents begin a destructive, vengeful cycle.

My ability to put some emotional distance between Heather's behavior and myself was instrumental in helping me during those devastating times. I learned to emotionally deal with her as if she had some terrible illness like leprosy. Uncontrolled leprosy can make a person very unpleasant to be around. He will look, smell, and act dreadfully, and in his discomfort he can cause others agonizing pain. Heather didn't have leprosy, but she was suffering, and she definitely was unpleasant to be around.

If a child with leprosy were causing his parents unbelievable anguish, they wouldn't strike back or abandon him. Instead they would maintain their focus on him, not his disease (or in Heather's case, her behavior), and they would do whatever was necessary to make him well. Doing this with Heather took practice. Because my heart often was bruised and broken, I worked on responding with my head, knowing that in time my heart would follow. As with learning to ride a bicycle, with time and practice I got better and better at it.

Show Challenging Kids Unconditional Love by . . .

■ **Separating the child from the behavior.**
Children should always be loved for who they are, not for what they do. Parents accomplish this by separating the child from the behavior.

■ **Doing it with your head, not your heart.**
Sometimes parents feel immobilized by the pain. However, unconditional love starts simply by making a cognitive choice to love.

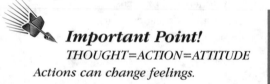

Important Point!
THOUGHT=ACTION=ATTITUDE
Actions can change feelings.

Betty was struggling with her thirteen-year-old daughter, Linda. They disagreed about almost everything, and Betty finally admitted there was little she liked about her rebellious teen. After attending a PWOP workshop, she wrote of the transformation that had taken place.

> I can't believe the change! As we worked on her unacceptable behavior using the PWOP strategy, I commented on her good behavior, pointed out her good qualities and literally forced myself to hug her. At first she didn't respond, but slowly she started turning around. Today, we actually enjoy each other and get along! I realize now the change had to start with me and it was a choice that I had to make. Actions really do change attitudes . . . hers and mine!

BEHAVIORAL WAYS TO SHOW UNCONDITIONAL LOVE

Walking children through tough times involves learning some basic communication techniques that perhaps have been overlooked. In his excellent book *How to Really Love Your Teenager*, Dr. Ross Campbell differentiates between verbal and behavioral orientation. Adults, he explains, can effectively communicate verbally because they're verbally oriented. Children, on the other hand, are not. They're more behaviorally oriented. Saying to your child all the things that create warm, fuzzy feelings is great and needs to be done often, but it's not enough. According to Campbell, the two most effective ways to communicate love to your child are through eye contact and appropriate physical contact.

Yes, we really do communicate with our eyes. Often our eyes act like windows to our emotions and our feelings. Campbell states,

> Without realizing it, you use eye contact to express many feelings — sadness, anger, hate, pity, rage and love. In some homes, there is amazingly little contact between parents and teenagers. What exists usually is negative, as when the teen is being reprimanded or given specific instructions.[1]

How sad to think that we look at our children only when we're telling them to do something, or when we're unhappy about something they have done. Many parents will probably stop here and say, "Wait a minute! I talk to my child and look at her when I do!" But do you really? Much of the conversation that takes place with children happens when parents are doing something else.

Many times Heather and I talked, all right, but I also did something else at the same time. I finished up paperwork in my office, washed dishes, or just straightened up the house. Looking back, I realize how frustrating it must have been for her. It was as if I said, "That's nice, dear, but not really important enough for me to give you my undivided attention."

When I realized the importance of this, I worked on taking the time to stop what I was doing, look her in the eyes, hang on to every word, and communicate. I also made sure my body language said, "I enjoy spending this time with you." And finally, I worked on treating her as I would my very best friend. By doing these things, I validated her worth and importance to me. As Heather's parents, we took this step first in a conscious effort to envelop Heather in our unconditional love. Again, it wasn't so much what we said but what we did as her parents.

Another great way to show a child unconditional love is through appropriate physical contact. Dr. Ross Campbell stresses the importance of touching your children physically.

> Appropriate and consistent physical contact is a vital way to give your teenager that feeling and conviction that you truly care about him. This is especially true when your teen is noncommunicative, sullen, moody, or resistant. During these times, eye contact may be difficult or impossible. But physical contact can almost always be used effectively.[2]

Parents really can touch their child's heart by appropriately touching her. This might be a slight back rub, a toss of her hair, a friendly pat on her shoulder or hand, or even a foot massage. Although it may seem insignificant, parents are sending a powerful message to their teen. They're communicating, "You're important to me and worthy of my interest and my time."

If your kids are younger, make sure you're doing this and then don't stop as they enter their teen years. Just be cautious as to where and when. For example, they'll appreciate it more if you hug them in the privacy of the car before they get out to meet their friends.

As Heather had grown older, I had stopped tucking her in bed at night. When I started looking for opportunities to touch her and tell her how much I loved her, I resurrected this bedtime ritual. I waited until she was just dozing off. As I sat on the side of her bed, pulled the covers up snugly around her shoulders, and stroked her hair, I told her how very special she was and how much she was loved by her father and me. And then I always added other comments, such as "You're very special to me," "I'm glad you're my kid," "Today was a better day than yesterday," "Things are going to be better . . . I promise," and "Heather, please don't give up on us, because we are never giving up on you."

THREE INTEGRAL PARTS TO A PERSON'S SELF-ESTEEM

Maurice Wagner, in his book *The Sensation of Being Somebody*, talks of three integral parts to a person's self-esteem: feeling you belong, feeling you're worthwhile, and feeling you're capable. Parents should incorporate these into their everyday lives with their children. According to Dr. Wagner, "Feeling you belong starts and stops at home. It's that feeling you get when you know that you're loved, cared for, wanted, enjoyed and you belong."[3]

Making an out-of-control child feel he belongs can be very difficult (especially when half the time you can't stand the sight of him), yet it's crucial to his emotional well-being. These challenging kids often perceive parental anger and frustration as rejection. Unfortunately, many times this results in alienating them even more from the family. Kids who become involved in gang activity are desperately looking for a place to belong and be accepted. University of Houston sociologists recently conducted a study on teen gangs that confirmed this. They found the primary reasons for joining gangs were to feel accepted and needed.[4]

As much as possible, we want to pull these kids back into the family and let them know that they're cared for, enjoyed, loved, and accepted at home. Again, this can be difficult, but it can be made easier by separating the child from his behavior.

Only after grasping the importance of this were we finally able to make steady progress in our relationship with Heather. When it was all said and done, we realized her behavior had nothing to do with the love we felt for her or what she meant to us. Much like the leper, Heather was miserable. And because of her pain and unhappiness, she was making those around her unhappy as well. But just like the parent coping with a child with leprosy, my focus wasn't on the horrific disease, but rather on its healing. In doing so, I was able to truthfully say, "I love you, Heather, simply because you're a person of immeasurable worth and you belong to me."

We often used grounding as a consequence for Heather when she was a young teenager. If she was grounded, however, she was never separated from the family. On many occasions, I used this as an opportunity for us to spend time together. Because Heather loved hats, we spent hours at the mall trying them on. True, I wasn't the friends she wanted to hang out with. But I was better than no one, and this gave us a time to connect emotionally.

An interesting thing takes place once children truly begin to feel they belong. Because they feel loved, they begin to believe that they're worthy of being loved, and consequently begin to feel that they're worthwhile. Dr. Wagner says this sense of worthiness deals primarily with self-acceptance: "Worthiness is a feeling of 'I'm good' or 'I count' or 'I'm right.'"[5] It's the one thing that enables you to look in the mirror, like what you see, and feel significant.

Needing to feel important is another reason teens say they get involved in gangs, according to the University of Houston study.[6] Make sure you treat your child with importance and significance at home. Ask him for his thoughts or advice on a particular subject. Talk with him as you would a friend.

Finally, Dr. Wagner stresses the importance of feeling capable or competent: "This is a feeling of adequacy, of courage, or hopefulness, of strength enough to carry out the task of daily life-situations. It's the 'I can' feeling of being able to face life and cope with its complexities."[7] The feeling of being capable is closely related to past successes in solving problems.

Initially, we'd helped Heather link her behavior with decisions she'd made. Up until this time, our focus had been only on bad behavior resulting from bad choices. We failed to see that she was making good decisions as well. We began to use the *Parenting Without Pressure* workbook to comment when she completed daily stuff, followed through on contracts, obeyed family rules, and even when she didn't repeat bad behavior. Knowing that she was capable of making good choices and doing things right helped her gain self-confidence. And because this resulted in Heather feeling good about herself, it was something she wanted to repeat.

The feeling of competence is developed from having successes, both big and small. As a child masters the small steps, enlarge his steps accordingly. Always make sure those steps are enough to challenge, but never so big that they overwhelm him.

ADDITIONAL WAYS TO SHOW UNCONDITIONAL LOVE

Unconditional love says to a child that I love you for who you are, not for what you do. Parents can effectively communicate that in the following ways:

- Appreciate the uniqueness of a child even when she has little in common with other family members. Kids don't have to be clones of Mom or Dad. Unfortunately, this can be troublesome for some parents. It's helpful to remember that your friends are usually friends because you have something in common. However, it's quite possible to have a child, one of your very own, with whom you have little in common. This situation doesn't automatically make one of you right and one wrong. It simply means you're different.

- Don't assign importance to only those attributes that you hold dear, like being thin, playing a particular sport, or being mechanical. Instead, help each child recognize his own uniqueness. How can you value your child's right to be whatever he wishes to be without always agreeing with his choice? Again, the "You Can Say Yes If You Can Say No" technique is outlined in the box below.

> ### You Can Say Yes If You Can Say No to . . .
>
> - Is this illegal?
> - Is this immoral?
> - Is it going to make a difference in five years?
> - Is this something that is going to hurt this child or somebody else?
> - Is it inappropriate for his age?

Be patient with your children's impatience. Be patient with their tendency to label you as old-fashioned. It's amazing how modern you'll become in a few short years. Mark Twain once said, "When I was a boy of fourteen, my father was so ignorant I could hardly stand to have the old man around. But, when I got to be twenty-one, I was astonished at how much he had learned in seven years." Review the different adolescent developmental stages. Remember that your child's impatience really has little to do with you. So don't take it personally.

Finally, parents should do whatever is necessary to encourage a child's belief in himself. Never see a child as a problem, but only as a challenge. Help him be all he can be. As we see our children, they'll see themselves. Psychologist William Glasser writes, "Children find in the eyes of their parents the mirror in which they define themselves in the relationship. Fill it with nothing, they become nothing. They have a tremendous ability to live down to the lowest expectation in any environment."[8]

Once I realized the importance of this, I consciously made sure that when Heather looked at me, I reflected the very best in her, as well as all the wonderful possibilities of what she could be.

If Dad doesn't live here anymore, does that mean we're not a family?

IMPROVING ON THE FAMILY

Redefining Families

I'll never forget the sorrow in the voice of a mom as she told a group of parents that because of her divorce, she and her boys were no longer going to be a family. She was certain that the reality of family life would gradually disappear. Unfortunately, for her the word *family* meant having a mom and a dad and 3.2 kids living under the same roof, with a van in the garage and a dog in the doghouse.

Many families no longer consist of the stereotypical husband, wife, three kids, and a dog, all living on the same property. Because of the increase in divorce and the growing number of children born to single parents, families today are defined simply as all the people who live in the same household. Ideally, however, they're committed to one another, spend time together, and share values, beliefs, warm memories, and family traditions. Here are a few statistics that show the changing characteristics of American families:

Single-parent families. There has been a 200 percent increase in single-parent families since 1970. Forty percent of all children will live with a single parent before they're eighteen. Approximately 25 percent of American children live in mother-only families.[9]

Blended families. A blended or stepfamily is one in which at least one of the adult partners has children from a prior relationship. According to The Stepfamily Association of America, thirteen hundred new stepfamilies are formed daily. The U.S. Census Bureau notes that nearly ten million children live in blended families.[10] Likewise, the government estimates that stepfamilies will outnumber traditional nuclear families by 2007.[11]

Missing Dad. Having a good relationship with Dad is important for a teenager's adjustment. However, twenty-five million children are growing up without fathers.[12] University of North Carolina sociologist Peter Uhlenberg reports that, sadly, one out of three teenagers has completely lost contact with his or her father after the parents got a divorce. Only 11 percent of kids with divorced parents frequently have contact with Dad.[13]

Grandparents. U.S. Census figures show that more than three million children in the United States live with grandparents and other relatives. In one million of those homes, grandparents are the primary caregivers to the grandchildren or great-grandchildren.[14]

Parental Commitment of Time

People spend time doing things they find most important. Or to put it a slightly different way: you make the time to do the things you really want to do.

Yet often, children get very little of their parents' time. According to a Pennsylvania State University study, working mothers spend a weekly average of 6.6 hours bathing, feeding, reading to, and playing with their children. Working fathers spend 2.5 hours and nonemployed dads spend 2.6 hours bathing, feeding, reading, and playing. And for those moms who feel guilty about working, this startling statistic was discovered: mothers who don't work outside the home average only 12.9 hours doing the same.[15]

On an average, parents spend 40 percent less time with their kids now than thirty years ago.[16] And yet for all teens, it turns out, the steady presence of an adult to provide support and positive values is the best guarantee of a happy, successful passage to adulthood.[17]

How Well Do You Know Your Child?

- What is his favorite color?
- What is her favorite food?
- What is his favorite subject at school?
- Where is his favorite place to go?
- What is her favorite restaurant?
- What is her best friend's name?

Unfortunately, today many busy parents tend to buy instead of to spend; that is, they buy games, toys, and other things for their children instead of spending time with them. "I can't be with you, but I'll buy you something when I get home" are words children today often hear.

Unstructured time. It takes time to get to know a young person, to feel her hurts and understand her problems. Parents continually need to look for opportunities to talk with their children, grabbing any chance they can find to share the lives of their kids. The key here is availability.

For Heather and me, the opportunity often came late at night. When Heather came in from a date, she was required to wake us up if we were asleep, as we usually were. Unfortunately for me, this was often the time she wanted to talk. Because I was determined not to miss my chance, we would sit at the kitchen table, laughing and talking well into the night. The mornings I left for work a little tired were a small price to pay for the late-night talks that have provided us both with some very warm memories.

Someone once said that love is spelled T-I-M-E. Time spent with children is an investment parents will never regret. Think of opportunities you might have to spend unstructured time with your children.

Structured time and making memories. In addition to grabbing every opportunity to spend unstructured time together, we also need to schedule time for the family. Spending time together provides the opportunity for happy memories from which the family can draw during difficult times.

In their excellent book *Crisis Proof Your Teenager*, Charles Wibbelsman and Kathleen McCoy state, "Memories that last—and carry us through the trying times of adolescence and beyond—are usually of the simple everyday variety. Quite often they're treasure gifts of parental time and attention."[18] These might include summer picnics, backyard barbecues, or even learning a sport together as a family.

Yet few families spend time together. In fact, I was surprised to learn that many families do only two things together: they clean the house and mow the grass. Upon examining my own family, I realized that although we were a little better at family times than that, we did leave a great deal to chance.

Spontaneity is great. Few family times, however, result from last-minute planning. Family times need to be scheduled, something everyone in the family knows about and can prepare for. Preparation is especially handy with reluctant teenagers. Use arbitration as an opportunity to discuss and plan a monthly family time. Make it a priority and put it on the calendar.

Heather went through a stage when she didn't like going on family outings. Giving her time to mentally prepare helped greatly. And because Heather was a child capable of raining on a parade, we built in an incentive for her to have fun with the family. For every time she went with us and got along with other family members, she could bring a friend on the next outing. The interesting thing about Heather's reluctance to spend time with the family is that I don't ever remember her having a bad time.

Suggestions for Family Fun

Rent videos.	Go to a ballgame.
Play board games.	Rollerblade together.
Go bowling.	Go to the beach or park.
Cook together.	Put together a puzzle.
Make homemade ice cream.	Go to a movie.
Go to the zoo.	Play putt-putt golf.
Work on an art or craft project.	Have a family reunion.
Go to a concert.	Play catch.
Go fishing.	Shoot baskets.
Throw a family party. Everyone	Build a snowman or sandcastle.
gets to invite two guests.	Go for a walk.
Go to a flea market.	Ride bikes.

Establishing Traditions

Family traditions don't have to be old-fashioned or elaborate affairs. In fact, a family tradition can be very simple. The trick is discovering something that is relevant to your family and works for you. Sometimes the warmest memories come from the simplest activities, such as preparing a special meal, going to Christmas Eve candlelight services, spending a day at the fair, celebrating promotions or school honors, working at the school carnival, or creating a special birthday celebration. Jennifer Allen writes in her article titled "The Incredible Healing Power of Family Rituals" that "the best rituals are really nothing more than a reflection of our desire to be close to one another."[19]

By having family fun times and establishing family traditions, parents make the time for sharing and recognize the importance of belonging to the family. Celebrating the family builds hopefulness and cements family ties.

You can start by identifying and celebrating your family's current traditions. Paul and Leisa Tigpen suggest in the book *52 Simple Ways to Build Family Traditions* that you categorize them under these headings:[20]

- *Seasonal traditions.* Is there a special way you celebrate holidays such as Christmas or Easter?
- *Traditions for special times of the day and week.* This might include going to church on Sunday or out to breakfast on Saturday morning.
- *Traditions for family milestones.* A bar mitzvah or bat mitzvah is an excellent example of celebrating a family member's milestone.
- *Traditions for celebrating your family achievements*. A good report card might warrant a special dinner or cake.
- *Traditions for honoring and serving one another.* Birthday or anniversary celebrations honor family members.

MAKING STEPFAMILIES WORK

When Henry and Libby Tucker recently attended a PWOP workshop, they were at the point of separation. In a brief eighteen-month period their blended family of three children (hers) had digressed from one big happy family and "please treat my children just like your own" to screaming matches of "you're not my dad" and "don't tell my kids what to do!"

Their love for one another was apparent. But the frustration they were experiencing with the children and each other was definitely eroding the relationship.

They'd made many mistakes, but they admitted their biggest was that they didn't understand the dynamics of stepfamily life. They quickly learned, however, that the challenge of blending families can bring great rewards with understanding, hard work, and realistic expectations.

Understand the Process

This starts by understanding the process. For example, stepfamilies differ from former nuclear families because they're built on loss. The emotions experienced often parallel that of marriages that have ended in death. Hence, before remarriage, it's essential to work through the grieving process. Getting stuck in any one of these stages can result in unresolved anger and guilt that make a successful remarriage very difficult.

Children often experience the greatest loss. A child's emotional transition can be the rockiest. Many not only lose daily contact with their noncustodial parent, but they also may lose neighborhood friends and schoolmates because of a move. It's easy for these kids to mask their pain with anger and defiant behavior. Don't react to their inappropriate behavior. Instead, remain emotionally connected, empathize with their feelings, and help mourn their loss. Also, let your child know that divorce is an adult problem. Finally, provide as much stability as possible. If possible, maintain the same school, activities, and schedule.

Justin, Libby's eleven-year-old son, hadn't seen his dad in three years and missed him terribly. Although he admitted he liked Henry, he was quick to point out that Henry wasn't his dad and he couldn't tell him what to do! This often left Henry feeling frustrated and very unappreciated.

Understand the Stages

Understanding the different stages a blended family experiences eliminates the element of surprise and helps keep expectations realistic. Each of the stages brings with it individual emotional growth as well as changes in the way family members relate to one another. On an average, this evolutionary process can take anywhere from one-and-a-half to two years.

In her excellent book *Stepfamily Realities,* Margaret Newman suggests that stepfamilies move through five predictable growth stages: The Fantasy Stage, The Confusion Stage, The Conflict Stage, The Coming-Together Stage, and The Resolution Stage.

The Fantasy Stage

- Everybody is on his or her best behavior.
- This stage is known as the "Brady Bunch" period, because everyone imagines loving one another, being one big happy family, and living happily ever after.
- Subconsciously, the parent often sees herself as being rescued and the stepparent sees himself as shaping up the household.

The Confusion Stage

- The romantic phase of the marital relationship appears to end.
- Growing tension causes previously experienced happiness to slip away.
- There is typically a denial of many signs of pending trouble.

The Conflict Stage

- Family members become aware that their needs are not being met and can behave aggressively.
- Power struggles ensue.
- This stage must be skillfully negotiated for stepfamily maturity to be achieved. Unfortunately, families get stuck in this stage with years of conflict and strife. Therefore, many families turn to counseling to get back on track.

The Coming-Together Stage

- Emotions become less intense.
- Family members learn how to resolve issues.
- Although relationships are not ideal, there's a growing awareness among family members that they're a family.

The Resolution Stage

- There's relief that the bad times have passed.
- Family members are more able to be themselves and accept each other for better or worse.
- Optimism returns and the future looks better.[21]

When they arrived at the PWOP workshop, the Tuckers were definitely stuck in the Confusion and Conflict stages. Never having had children, Henry was at a loss when dealing with Libby's.

First and foremost, Henry had unrealistic expectations. Upon marrying Libby, he assumed the kids would love and accept him as their "new" dad. Needless to say, they were quick to point out that he wasn't their dad.

Also, Henry had a tendency to personalize their behavior. The children's ages ranged from eleven to fifteen and much of what Henry was experiencing was typical of adolescents. However, he was sure it was directed at him.

Emotions Children Experience Following Remarriage

Grief: Remarriage results in a loss and it's natural to grieve.

Fear: Children lose their sense of order and they fear they no longer fit in. Also, they're most concerned about what is going to happen to them.

Jealousy: It can be hard sharing living space and possessions, much less a parent, with a stepparent or stepsiblings.

Guilt: Many children blame themselves for the breakup of their parents' marriage and feel disloyal if they accept and enjoy their stepparent.

Finally, immediately after their marriage Henry became the primary disciplinarian. At first, Libby was grateful for the respite, but as the children's resentment grew she often would side with the kids and create a real "us versus him" problem.

BUILDING A SUCCESSFUL STEPFAMILY

True, blending a family is hard work. As with all families, there are periods of adjustments, changes, behavioral ups and downs, and good days and bad. However, you can set yourself up with more ups than downs and more good days than bad by remembering the following.

Some parents come with a lot of emotional baggage. This usually results when they have difficulty successfully resolving issues from prior marriages. Perhaps they haven't successfully worked through the grieving process and are stuck in one of the stages. This often results in the lack of an emotional divorce. The blended family then gets slam-dunked with the leftover emotional baggage of resentment, anger, and hostility. Parents should avoid displacing feelings by identifying them and determining their source. Seek professional counseling if you're experiencing difficulty resolving issues from the past.

Libby's ex-husband had been emotionally abusive and often verbally abused the kids to hurt her. So when Henry attempted to discipline the kids, Libby experienced the unresolved feelings of anger and resentment. With the help of counseling, she realized that much of the anger she experienced was left over from her first marriage.

While the different stages in blending families are fairly predictable, at each stage families can experience elements of other stages (such as conflict). By understanding and being realistic about each stage, parents can be prepared to successfully navigate through them.

The Tuckers were greatly relieved once they understood the aspects of the different stages. Realizing they weren't alone and that they could learn to navigate the different stages gave them hope.

Communication is the key to successful stepfamilies. Family meetings are a great help as they allow the family to stay on track. They also enable parents to effectively deal with problematic areas when they're small. More important, meetings give stepchildren an opportunity to be heard and have needs met.

Weekly family meetings eliminated much of the daily tension and strife the Tuckers were experiencing. Also, Henry felt more included in family decision making.

To discipline effectively, you must first establish a positive relationship with the stepchild. Dr. James Bay, a clinical psychologist, says that "it takes typically two to four years before a stepchild accepts a stepparent in the parental role. They should respect you and you can tell them what to do, but don't discipline them."[22] You can begin to build a good relationship by spending time alone together. For example, you can drive your stepchildren to activities such as baseball practices or dance lessons and then stop for ice cream on the way home. The key is to make yourself emotionally available and then wait for the child to come to you.

Because Henry went into the marriage with the idea he could shape the kids up, it was hard for him to let go in this area.

Make Children Feel Special and Significant

- Spend time alone with them.
- Share daily activities so you can talk.
- Use school work, TV, and music as a springboard to conversation.
- Get involved in their activities.
- Learn to listen—really listen.

However, by using the PWOP strategy he was able to back off and focus on his relationship with his stepchildren. For example, knowing that Justin liked to fish, Henry planned fishing trips for the two of them.

PWOP Can Help

The *Parenting Without Pressure* program ensures the biological parent success in taking the lead with discipline. This parenting strategy creates a safe format to determine rules, consequences, and operating boundaries. It also provides a platform to address everyone's needs. Moreover, no one individual ends up being the heavy. This allows the stepparent to be a supportive participant with discipline while everyone adjusts to new family rules and roles. Also, because of the tangible workbook system and weekly family meetings, everyone knows what to expect every time.

Never put a child in a position of defending his biological parent. The biological parent might be many things, but he will always be the child's parent. By making negative statements about the biological parent, you only make the child angry and hurt. Even if the statements are true, you'll always put that child in a position where he feels he must defend that parent.

Tips for Stepparents

- Relationships take time. Show acceptance and be honest, reasonable, and fair. Aim to be a friend rather than a parent.
- Discipline only after you've established a positive relationship with your step-children. Before that, be supportive of the biological parent's discipline.
- Children can be unappreciative and unpleasant as they adjust. Don't take their behavior personally.
- Keep realistic expectations and maintain a positive, healthy attitude.
- Acknowledge the children's relationship with their other parent. Never undermine that relationship or the other parent.
- Love cannot be legislated. Loving or being loved by your stepchildren never happens immediately.
- Treat all family members with genuine courtesy and respect.

Both Henry and Libby had difficulty in this area. They were often resentful of Libby's ex-husband's lack of financial or emotional commitment to the children and would verbalize similarities when they noted irresponsible behavior in the kids. When they realized how damaging and destructive this was, both Henry and Libby apologized to the kids. Moreover, they made a commitment to keep negative comments to themselves. Henry also became more civil by treating Libby's ex-spouse with courtesy and respect when they met.

Don't hesitate to seek outside help when problems reach crisis levels. It's not unusual for things to get a little ugly during the Confusion and Conflict stages. Getting stuck here, however, can lead to years of lose/lose situations for everyone.

Counseling and a stepfamily support group continue to provide the Tuckers with information and needed support. Also, they're learning skills to prevent problems from reaching crisis levels. Recently, Henry said, "We're no longer not just putting out fires but learning how not to start them!"

Schedule family times together and just have fun. This will provide an opportunity to enhance family communication and build family intimacy. In addition to combining family traditions already in place, celebrate your family by establishing traditions that are unique to your new family.

Besides having a weekly date night, the Tuckers scheduled a monthly family fun night. Henry also made individual "dates" with the kids.

A parent's best bet?

1. Understand the different stages of the stepfamily.

2. Maintain open lines of communications, hold weekly family meetings, and spend time building relationships with each of the children.

3. Distribute all resources fairly among the children.

4. Make sure visiting stepchildren have a place in your home to call their own.

5. Seek outside help when tough problems arise.

6. Treat all family members with civility.

7. Celebrate together and have fun.

MAKING HOME A SAFE PLACE

During the past twenty years, this country has seen a dramatic shift in things we consider entertaining and enjoyable. The biggest change has occurred in TV programming. Gone are programs such as *Little House on the Prairie* and *The Mary Tyler Moore Show.* They've been replaced by *Jerry Springer* and *South Park.* The basic civility of treating one another with courtesy and respect has given way to bad manners and the "dis" mentality of being mean and rude. Dr. James Garbarino notes that this shift provokes a callousness that generalizes into other relationships.[23]

The home needs to be a physical and emotional safe-place for all the family members. Parents can start by protecting children from messages that teach violence (in either speech or action) as an acceptable means for conflict resolution. Carefully screen TV, music, and video games kids watch, play, and listen to.

Establish family guidelines that prohibit pushing, shoving, or hitting by any family member. Physical aggression reinforces the notion that "might makes right"—a lose/lose concept for both children and parents.

Additionally, everyone should be required to treat the others with respect. No exceptions! No one should ever be allowed to have a good time at the expense of another.

Like parents, children should not be allowed to emotionally abuse one another. Unfortunately, some parents who immediately would step in and stop *physical* combat between children often allow siblings to *verbally* obliterate one another. Verbal attacks may not cause physical injury, but they can bruise the spirit and can cause wounds that last a lifetime.

Parents aren't going to be able to eliminate bickering among children. But they can discourage jealousy and unhealthy competition and should never tolerate a verbal onslaught.

Teach your children that picking on each another is not an appropriate substitute for dealing with disagreements or eliminating boredom. More important, send a strong message that it won't be tolerated.

A mother who recently attended a PWOP workshop had an excellent idea for eliminating the verbal bashing that was going on between her children. She simply established a "no knock" rule. She charged fifty cents for every belittling or unkind statement that one child directed toward another. She followed through with the rule by having the child who was on the receiving end of the hurtful statement write in his workbook exactly what was said, who said it, and the time and date on which it was said. When allowances were paid on arbitration day, the mother deducted fifty cents for that statement from the allowance of the offending child.

What a great idea! The first week this rule was implemented, twelve dollars changed hands. By the second week, the kids had caught on and only two dollars changed hands. And soon her children were giving careful thought to what they said.

Another mom required the child who said the offending statement to write, "I will treat *(child's name)* with courtesy and respect," fifty, one hundred, or 150 times. The amount would depend on the offender's age and difficulty learning the lesson. For example, for the first offense he would write fifty times, second he would write one hundred times, and third he would write 150.

Teach your children constructive ways for dealing with disagreements with one another. Remind them that arbitration is an excellent means for conflict resolution. For example, in many households with teenage girls, there is usually an ongoing conflict about clothes. My own teenage daughters were often caught in the conflict of what belonged to whom and who borrowed what. Instead of threats and harsh words, they hashed it out at arbitration and got everything back into the right closets.

Set this up to be a win/win proposition. Encourage your children to cooperate with one another, to get along and be team players. If a week goes by without any verbal bashing among family members, celebrate. Take the family to a movie or out for pizza. Again, set up the family to win. If verbal bashing has been ongoing behavior between the children in your family, start changing that by taking it a day at a time. And when they make it through a whole day without any verbal bashing, celebrate.

Remember, positively reinforced behavior is destined to be repeated. Most of the discord between youngsters is the result of sibling rivalry, much of which is to be expected. But as parents, you can help reduce it. Continually strive to hold each family member in high regard. Be careful not to single out one particular attribute of a child that you personally favor, such as playing a sport or making good grades. Instead, recognize each child for his or her special talents and qualities.

Appendix A

■ ■ ■

THE FAMILY WORKBOOK

Worksheets for the family

Things to Discuss at Arbitration

Date:

1. _____

2. _____

3. _____

4. _____

Date:

1. _____

2. _____

3. _____

4. _____

Daily Stuff

Date: _____

Please complete: _____

1. _____

2. _____

3. _____

4. _____

Messages: _____

_____

_____

_____

_____

_____

_____

_____

_____

_____

_____

_____

_____

_____

_____

Daily Stuff

My Jobs	Monday	Tuesday	Wednes.	Thursday	Friday	Saturday	Sunday

Notes:

Fun Times and Evenings Out

Date: _____

Time leaving/returning: _____

Where I'll be: _____

_____

Friends I'll be with: _____

_____

_____

Date: _____

Time leaving/returning: _____

Where I'll be: _____

_____

Friends I'll be with: _____

_____

_____

Date: _____

Time leaving/returning: _____

Where I'll be: _____

_____

Friends I'll be with: _____

_____

_____

Friends and Family

Emergency Numbers

Police: 911   Fire: 911   Rescue Unit: 911

Family Doctor: _____

Parents and Relatives:

Mom at work: _____

Dad at work: _____

Relative: _____

Relative: _____

Parents' Friends:

Name and number: _____

Name and number: _____

Name and number: _____

Neighbors:

Name and number: _____

Name and number: _____

Name and number: _____

My Friends and Their Parents:

Friend's name and number: _____

Friend's parent cell number: _____

Friend's name and number: _____

Friend's parent cell number: _____

Friend's name and number: _____

Friend's parent cell number: _____

Friend's name and number: _____

Friends

NAME: _____

Friend's Name:	Parents' Names:	Phone Number:

My Child's Behavior

I like	I dislike

Rules We Can Live By

NAME: _____

Behavior: _____

_____

Rule: _____

Consequence/Incentive: _____

_____

_____

Behavior: _____

_____

Rule: _____

Consequence/Incentive: _____

_____

_____

Behavior: _____

_____

Rule: _____

Consequence/Incentive: _____

_____

_____

Arbitration Worksheet

1. Define the problem. _____

_____

_____

  Can we stop here? _____

2. Let the kids talk. _____

_____

_____

3. Let the parents talk. _____

_____

_____

4. Brainstorm possible solutions. _____

_____

_____

5. Choose the best solution. _____

_____

_____

6. How did it go? _____

_____

_____

Weekly Progress Report

Name: _____

For week of: _____

Class	Subject	Teacher	GPA
1st period			
2nd period			
3rd period			
4th period			
5th period			
6th period			

Family Contract

Name: _____

Subject: _____

Desired Behavior: _____

How it will be accomplished: _____

_____

_____

_____

_____

_____

Consequences and/or incentives: _____

_____

_____

_____

_____

_____

_____

_____

Child's Signature: _____   Date: _____

Parent's Signature: _____   Date: _____

Appendix B

■ ■ ■

QUESTIONS PARENTS ASK

More information on using the workbook

For additional help getting started, I've included some of the most common questions about the workbook.

Q. Who writes in the children's workbooks and where do parents keep their notes?
A. Both parents and children write in the workbooks. Parents assign chores and write notes in "Daily Stuff." They also utilize "Anything and Everything Goes" to list arbitration topics. Kids use sections 1 through 4 to write their rules, list their friends, sign out before going out for the evening, and write notes to Mom and Dad. The important thing to remember, however, is that the workbook is simply a tool for the family. Use it in a way that works best for you!

Q. Can you use the program without making workbooks for your children?
A. Yes. Some families use a modified version that includes using responsibility/chore charts, and posting household rules and a family and friend's list on the computer. However, I recommend making the workbooks. It provides the structure and easy format to teach children the important concepts of accountability, responsibility, behavioral consequences, problem solving, and making good choices. Equally important, the workbook enables parents to easily shift their focus to what the children are doing right.

Q. Only one of our two children is giving us a tough time. Should we implement workbooks with both kids?
A. Yes. Not only does the workbook allow you to correct inappropriate behavior, it also serves as an excellent preventive tool for future problems.

Q. What age child is best suited for this program?
A. It works best with school-age children between the ages of six or seven and eighteen.

Q. Can you use the program with older kids who are in their late teens or early twenties? Our nineteen-year-old son needs it.
A. Absolutely. However, because of your son's age, I recommend that you use only the "Rules We Can Live By" and "Daily Stuff" sections. Also, weekly arbitrations are important.

After living on campus for three years, our daughter Heather moved back home during her senior year of college. Because she was an adult, we treated her as such. However, the workbook system again provided us with a safe structure. Everyone knew clearly what was expected. We had several basic household rules, and Heather was required to help with household chores that I assigned in the "Daily Stuff" section. Also, we consistently held weekly arbitrations to deal with small situations before they became big problems.

Q. When I suggested starting the program and workbook, my teenager just laughed. Now what?

A. Don't suggest. Inform your teen that you're going to implement the program and the workbook because you want to eliminate the fighting in your house. Also inform him that this program is fair because it deals with tangible measures and will give him more control over what he can and can't do.

Q. We have been implementing the workbook system for several months. However, many times my teenage son still doesn't remember to complete his daily stuff, which means I end up doing it. Any suggestions?

A. Determine why he's not completing his daily stuff. Are you being sensitive to his school schedule? Does he have adequate time? If his explanation is that he forgets, inform him that his memory lapse is no excuse and try the following: First, formulate a rule/consequence concerning daily stuff that includes a specific time for each task to be completed. Second, give other children in the family the opportunity to complete his assigned task for money (one dollar per item, which is then deducted from his allowance). If this generates discord among the kids, simply complete the task and pay yourself. Third, remind your son that this is an area of responsibility that will be examined at arbitration when he wants extended privileges.

Q. How do you handle a crisis situation that occurs during the week and your arbitration is on the weekend?

A. If possible, apply your disobeying rule. Heather's disobeying rule stated: "Any willful act of disobedience will result in being grounded until the next arbitration." At that meeting, we discussed the problem and, if needed, the additional consequence. This eliminated immediately addressing a serious problem when we felt angry and hadn't thought it through. However, if the crisis warrants immediate attention, take enough time to get your emotions in check and then call an emergency arbitration.

Q. What do you do if a child destroys his workbook or it disappears?

A. Always make the child responsible for his workbook. If it disappears, he's responsible for its replacement cost and for duplicating the information it contained. If he destroyed the workbook, then in addition to the above, either his disobeying rule with its consequence would apply or he could lose all TV and phone privileges for a week.

Q. Recently, I asked my daughter to do a few extra things that I hadn't included in her "Daily Stuff" section. She said she didn't have to do them because they were not on her list. Is she right?

A. The fairness of the program wins over kids more quickly than anything else.

Consequently, be as fair as possible. Imagine having your boss continually add to your list of assigned tasks. Just when you thought you were making progress, he adds several more items. That's how kids feel when you add to their lists. However, having said all that, you're the parent and you have the right to make additional requests. But the requests should be important, and I wouldn't do this often.

Q. Should we have workbooks for my husband's children when they stay with us every other weekend?

A. Probably not. You do have a right, however, to expect them to follow your household rules. Always make sure you've defined these rules before you enforce them. Additionally, if they are dating from your household, make sure you have a list of friends and that they sign out before going out.

Q. For years my son has fed his dog. Since we started the workbook system, he doesn't do it unless it's listed. Now what?

A. List feeding the dog as part of his daily stuff chores. Or give him the choice of feeding the dog with or without a rule and a consequence.

Appendix C

■ ■ ■

PARENTING PROBLEMS AND SOLUTIONS

Confronting the frequently asked questions

As I've taught *Parenting Without Pressure* workshops through the years, participants have frequently told me about their children's behavioral problems and asked for solutions. I've listened, helped brainstorm workable solutions—and learned that kids find creative ways to frustrate their parents!

On the following pages, I've described some problems and my suggestions for their resolution. Maybe you'll find yourself in a few of these situations, and hopefully the solutions will work for you. But remember, success depends on parents being firm and consistent with discipline while providing plenty of unconditional love.

Problem: Franchesca's Failing

Our eighth-grader is more interested in the social aspects of school than in the academics. How anyone can fail the eighth grade is beyond me. But that is where Franchesca's headed. Any suggestions?

Solution: Start by reviewing chapter 7. This will allow you to answer important questions such as what Franchesca is capable of academically, how she is physically, what is going on socially, and so on. If all you need is to ground your social butterfly, try this:

> RULE: "You must make a numerical GPA of 2.0 in each one of your classes for the week."

> CONSEQUENCE: "If you don't make a 2.0 GPA in each one of your classes for the week, you're grounded for the weekend."

> EXTRINSIC INCENTIVE: "For every 2.0 or better on your weekly progress report, we will add fifty cents to your allowance."

> INTRINSIC INCENTIVE: "Great grades! I knew you could do it. Wonderful! Boy, I can really see the hard work in this!"

Problem: Dora Doesn't Come Home

Because my daughter could no longer manage my fifteen-year-old granddaughter, Dora has been living with me for the past two years. Recently, she has started disappearing after school. She knows she's supposed to come straight home, but she's usually very vague and says she's just hanging out with friends or going to the mall. I don't get home from work until six. My sister Dorothy says she can help, but she's older, can't stand kids, and is meaner than a rattlesnake. Help!

Solution: Once kids know exactly what your household rules are, they need to be held accountable. By all means, take your sister up on her willingness to help. Establish a clear rule: "You must come straight home after school. No going to the mall, hanging out with friends, or stopping anywhere without permission." Attach a specific consequence: "If you don't come straight home from school, for the next week your Aunt Dorothy will pick you up from school and you'll stay with her at her house until I get off from work." Finally, always remember to reward behavior you want to have repeated. For example: "Thank you for coming straight home from school. I really appreciate it! It's wonderful being able to count on you."

Problem: Alex's Temper Tantrum

Alex has no regard for the personal property of others. Often when he's angry, he gets destructive. He punches holes in walls and breaks things. One time he became so furious with his sister that he broke my cellular phone by throwing it across the family room. Alex says he can't control his temper. I say he won't. What do you say?

Solution: I say Alex has a right to his feelings. However, he doesn't have the right to always act on them. At arbitration, talk to Alex about his anger.

Often underneath anger are the emotions of hurt, frustration, or fear. However, the only safe emotion for many boys to experience is anger with aggression. Also, anger is a safe way to mask feelings of being sad or lonely. Get to the heart of what is going on with Alex. Where is the intense emotion coming from?

Then suggest positive ways to control a flaring temper such as taking a walk or punching a punching bag. An anger management class might also be helpful.

Finally, carefully explain to Alex that you'll no longer tolerate his destructive behavior. Establish a rule that says, "If you throw a tantrum and damage other people's property, you'll make restitution and be grounded for a week." If Alex's destructive outbursts continue, seek professional help.

Finally, be sure to comment when Alex does act appropriately. For example: "I could see how frustrated you were with your sister. It showed me a lot of maturity when you left the room rather than reacting to her behavior. Thanks."

Problem: Sally's Disaster Area

To say Sally's bedroom is a wreck is an understatement. It looks more like a toxic-waste site. We fight about it constantly because I can't stand the mess. On several occasions, I got so frustrated that I cleaned it myself. My husband tells me to close the bedroom door and forget it. That's hard for me to do. I want the room cleaned up. What do you suggest?

Solution: I had a similar problem with Heather for years. But finally I hit on a solution. We wrote a rule that said, "Every morning before school, your bed must be made and all towels picked up and hung in the bathroom." As a consequence for not doing this, I charged Heather one dollar for an unmade bed and seventy-five cents per wet towel. During the week, I let everything else go. And as your husband suggested to you, I shut her bedroom door.

However, every Saturday I required Heather to clean her room. Because her idea of "clean" was different from mine, I developed a list of tasks to complete. For example: clean under and behind the bed; change the bed sheets; pick up everything on the floor and put it in the proper place; dust and straighten the top of the desk and dresser; vacuum the carpet; vacuum and organize the closet floor. Then after Heather cleaned, I checked the list to decide if the room looked satisfactory.

Problem: Shage's Shoplifting

Recently, the police arrested our fourteen-year-old daughter for shoplifting. Shage is a nice girl and has never been in trouble before. Needless to say, we're heartsick. What's the best way to deal with this?

Solution: As tough as it is, allow Shage to suffer the results of her actions. She must learn that her behavior has consequences and that most businesses prosecute to the fullest extent of the law for shoplifting.

Then determine the reason for Shage's behavior and specifically address the problem. Was she trying to gain peer acceptance? Kids who struggle with poor self-esteem are more vulnerable to negative peer pressure. Did she shoplift to get a "high" from doing it? Kids sometimes shoplift for excitement and the satisfaction of not getting caught. Was she stealing things her budget would not allow her to buy? Kids with limited resources sometimes steal items such as CDs or clothing. Or was she seeking attention and asking for help? Shoplifting is a red flag that says, "Something is wrong here. I need help." Shage may need professional counseling.

In addition to the legal consequences, I would apply your disobeying rule. Also, I would require Shage to write a 250- to 500-word essay about the many problems associated with retail theft. For example, according to Retailer's Association of America, we pay an additional 7 percent for every purchase just to cover the loss retailers incur from shoplifting. After Shage completes the essay, discuss with her what she's learned from this episode.

Problem: Lance's Constant Lies

My teenage son Lance lies so much, I never know when he's telling the truth. What should I do?

Solution: Explain to Lance that lying can become a habit, that it never pays, and that it destroys your trust. Then establish a rule and consequence about the lying.

More important, uncover why your child lies to you. For example, some kids from rigid, authoritarian homes feel they must lie to get breathing room. Or if Mom and Dad are quick to say no to friends and activities, kids may quit asking and start lying.

It's wiser for parents to say yes as much as possible and then work with their children on good decision making and trust building.

Children also lie because of poor self-esteem. They create fantasies that plug the holes in their fragile egos. For example, kids can tell elaborate tales to their friends just to impress them. Maybe Lance needs you to help build his self-esteem.

Other children lie to postpone punishment, especially when consequences aren't reasonable. Do your rules and consequences fit his age, personality, and circumstances?

And unfortunately, kids sometimes lie because their parents have taught them to. Check your own behavior. Have you modeled the message that lying is acceptable? For example, have you ever asked a family member to lie on your behalf? Or have your kids heard you lie to others? It's important to remember that kids learn more by watching your behavior than by listening to your verbal instructions.

Problem: Julie's Questionable Friends

Our daughter Julie is hanging out with some questionable kids. Her grades have dropped and lately she's been surly and disrespectful. My husband wants to snoop through her things. I think it would be an invasion of her privacy. What do you think?

Solution: For teenagers, privacy is a privilege, not a right. If she's behaving well, respect her privacy. However, if things are not going well, it's time to do a little investigating. If you want to know how your daughter is doing, first consider her best friend. Chances are, Julie is doing the same things as her friend.

If you suspect drug or alcohol abuse or other dangerous behavior, you need to look further. Going through a child's drawers, closet, and personal items is difficult, so please don't do it when everything is fine. But sometimes, for the sake of your child's life, it's a must.

Problem: Danny's Phantom Illness

Danny often complains of feeling sick on school days or when I've given him chores around the house. Ironically, he makes a remarkable recovery when he wants to do something with his friends in the evening. I feel he's manipulating me. What can I do about this?

Solution: Buy a thermometer and establish a rule that says, "Unless you have a temperature of one hundred degrees or more, you'll go to school or complete your assigned task. The only exception is if you're vomiting. If you do stay home from school or if you don't complete your assigned task because of illness, you'll need to rest. You won't be allowed to see your friends or go out with them on the days you stay home." This rule usually eliminates phantom illnesses.

Finally, I would address the underlying reason why Danny is having difficulty following through with chores or school. For example, often kids who are being teased or bullied at school will go to any lengths to avoid the confrontations.

Problem: Laurie's Door Slamming

Every time Laurie gets angry with someone in the family, she runs to her room, slams the door, and locks it. I don't mind Laurie going to her room, but when she slams the door, the entire house shakes. Any suggestions?

Solution: At arbitration, carefully explain to Laurie that slamming doors is no longer acceptable. Then simply establish a rule that says, "You may not slam doors." The consequence? Remove the door for a week.

Problem: Aaron's Bad Mouth

My son has a mouth you wouldn't believe! His swearing upsets me. Any suggestions?

Solution: Establish a rule that says, "No swearing allowed." Then make sure he understands what you consider to be swearing. The consequence would depend on your son's age. A younger child can write fifty to one hundred times, "I will not use profanity," or write a two-hundred-word essay on why he shouldn't swear. The assignment must be completed before he can eat dinner, which will be served at the dinner hour only. If the assignment isn't completed, he misses dinner.

For a teenager, charge five dollars per offending word. If his allowance doesn't cover the account balance, give him a list of chores and pay minimum wage for doing them.

Problem: Stacy's Slipping Out

I've just learned that Stacy, my sixteen-year-old daughter, is slipping out at night. Apparently she waits until everyone is asleep and then sneaks out her bedroom window. I don't want to permanently lock her bedroom windows in case of a fire, but what else can a parent do?

Solution: Let Stacy know that slipping out at night is a major breach of trust. As a consequence, for the next three weeks she'll be on restriction. Also inform her that from now on during the night you'll set your alarm and periodically check that she's in her room. If the problem continues, install an alarm system so every time a window or door opens at night, the alarm goes off.

Problem: Michelle's Phone Use

In your workshops, you mention that parents can revoke phone privileges as a consequence. We'd like to use this method with our daughter Michelle, but my husband and I don't get home until 6:30 in the evening. How can we enforce a phone restriction if we're not at the house in the afternoon? We have other children and don't want to remove the phone completely.

Solution: If Michelle has lost her phone privilege, you simply can ask her not to use the phone. Ideally, she will comply. However, a good consequence is one that you can enforce. Therefore, if Michelle doesn't comply, use something else that you can enforce, such as an earlier bedtime or loss of evening TV privileges.

Problem: Mandy's Refusal to Arbitrate

You suggest holding a weekly arbitration with children. However, every time I mention arbitration to my teenage daughter Mandy, she tells me to forget it.

Solution: This problem sounds similar to the situation of a mother who attended a *Parenting Without Pressure* workshop. She felt at a loss about how to involve her daughter in arbitration. The following solution worked well for her.

This mother told her daughter that she'd shop for groceries only after they successfully held a Saturday morning arbitration to establish household rules. Her daughter told her to forget it. Consequently, the mom didn't shop for groceries. Actually, this worked well for the mother because she wanted to lose some weight. Every morning on her way to work, she purchased two diet drink meal supplements, and on the way home she purchased a diet meal and a salad from the deli.

After a few days when the bread, milk, and cereal disappeared, the daughter asked, "When are you going grocery shopping?" The mom replied, "I don't know? When are we going to have an arbitration?"

The daughter held out longer and when the soup, Spam, and sardines in the back of the pantry were gone, she asked again, "When are you going to get groceries?" Her mother answered, "It's up to you. When are we going to have an arbitration?" The teen held out for ten days and finally felt ready to talk.

One word of caution: Parental attitude is very important. Make sure you're communicating this: "I love you and arbitration can work for both of us."

Problem: Jason's Morning Tardiness

My eight-year-old, Jason, constantly makes me late for work. I can't get him out of bed on time. And because he takes his sweet time and dawdles, I end up frustrated and screaming at him. I'm at a loss for what to do.

Solution: Inform your son that you're no longer going to be late for work. From now on, you'll leave the house at exactly 8:00 in the morning and whatever shape he's in at that time is the way he'll go to school. Make a list of things he must accomplish before breakfast, such as washing his face, brushing his teeth, getting dressed, combing his hair, and making his bed. Allow him to put a big check by each accomplished task, and if he accomplishes all of them, give him a token. When he acquires five tokens, take Jason to his favorite fast-food restaurant on Friday after school.

Recently, a mom who attended a *Parenting Without Pressure* workshop had a similar problem. But the son realized she meant business after he arrived at school with a shoe on one foot and only a sock on the other. Her son explained the sock by telling friends that he hurt his foot. After that experience, though, he got ready on time in the morning.

Problem: Toni's School Detentions

I carpool with several other middle school mothers. Toni, my thirteen-year-old daughter, constantly earns detentions for being late to class because she spends too much time talking with friends. Consequently, between the carpool and picking up Toni from detention, I spend the afternoon in my car. I'm tired of it! I've tried taking away her phone and it doesn't work. What do you suggest?

Solution: I'd give the problem back to Toni. You've already arranged daily transportation to and from school via the car pool. If because of her behavior Toni gets a detention, make her responsible for transportation home. Three options come to mind: (1) Toni can walk home, but you might not feel comfortable if the neighborhood isn't safe or if it's too far a walk. (2) She can call a cab and pay the fare from her allowance or by working for you at minimum wage. (3) Determine the cab fare and charge her that amount when a family member picks her up from school.

Problem: Dean and Darcy's Stuff

When my two teenagers, Dean and Darcy, return home from school, they start shedding their stuff at the door. Jackets, book bags, shoes, purses, hairbrushes. You name it; it's tossed in this corner and that. When I get home from work, the house is a wreck and I get angry. Is it too much to ask kids to pick up after themselves?

Solution: No, it's not too much to ask. But for most teens, picking up their things is a learned behavior. Establish a rule that says, "You must pick up your things and put them in your room. The consequence: if Mom picks up your things, they're hers for a week."

As you pick up your kids' belongings, place each item in a paper bag and staple the top shut. With a marker, write on each bag the owner's name and when that item will be returned. However, remember that a good consequence is one that works. If taking the item for a week doesn't work, try charging one or two dollars for each belonging. The amount can be deducted from an allowance, lunch money, or the money from a part-time job. Be sure and say something positive, however, when Dean and Darcy do pick up after themselves!

Problem: Benjamin's Scattered Toys

I have a similar problem, except it's not books and hairbrushes, but toys. The battle begins when I ask seven-year-old Benjamin to pick up his toys and put them away.

Solution: It sounds as though you're locked in a power struggle. Give up the struggle. Buy a kitchen timer. Then carefully explain to Benjamin that he has fifteen minutes to pick up his toys. Anything not picked up when the timer goes off gets put in a "Sunday box." Toys in this box can be reclaimed only on Sunday. In the meantime, work overtime on rewarding behavior that you want repeated. Every time he picks up his toys, thank him.

Problem: Jon's School Fights

My son Jon is a high school student who's frequently in fistfights at school, and he's already been suspended twice this year. Mr. Tough Guy then sits at home watching TV and eating me out of house and home. I'm afraid he's going to fail the ninth grade again. What can I do?

Solution: First, find out what's going on at school and determine why your son fights. Kids who chronically act out usually have a problem in at least one of several areas. For example, is he academically capable of doing the work? A teen who struggles with studies may go to any length to avoid admitting the problem. Socially, do other kids tease him? Or have they learned that Jon has a short fuse and so they bait him until he throws a punch? Is Jon wrestling with something related to home life and acting it out at school?

Talk with Jon about what causes him to fight. Then explain that fighting is not an appropriate way to deal with frustration and anger. Discuss other ways to resolve conflict and deal with anger such as walking away, counting to ten, talking with a teacher or guidance counselor, or calling you on the phone.

Then establish a rule and consequence about physical fighting that says, "You may not physically fight. If you do fight—and especially if you're suspended for fighting—you'll spend your days at home working." Chores might include yard work, painting, digging up a garden, cleaning the basement, cleaning the garage, or other manual labor.

In addition, I would make it worthwhile for him to effectively resolve his problems and not get suspended from school. Add an incentive: "For every week that you don't get in trouble at school and earn a 2.0 grade point average, I will . . . " Help him identify what it feels like to behave correctly. If the fighting continues, seek professional counseling.

Problem: Tracy Runs Away from Home

Tracy, who is fifteen years old, ran away from home two days ago and we're frantic. Things have been rough at home, but we didn't expect her to leave. What should we do?

Solution: Running away is serious and a big red flag for parents. Several steps should be taken immediately:

- Contact your child's friends and their parents as soon as possible. Most runaways travel fewer than ten miles from home and stay with friends. Ask Tracy's friends to notify you immediately if they hear from her. Let them know that she doesn't have permission to be anywhere but home.
- Notify the police. Provide them with a recent photo and description.
- Call the runaway organizations. Call the National Center for Missing and Exploited Children: 1-800-843-5678. This organization will provide you with immediate assistance in locating your child. Also contact the National Runaway Switchboard for counseling and referral services: 1-800-621-4000. Have someone stay by the phone with a pencil and paper in case Tracy calls you.

Once Tracy returns home and everyone calms down, you'll need to resolve the things that you describe as "rough at home." Identify the problem(s). Often children run away from something rather than to something. She may have run because of a breakdown in communication and constant fighting between her and you. She could feel like no one cares and that life at home is a big hassle to avoid. Or a family crisis could have motivated her to leave, such as alcohol or drug use, separation, divorce, death, or another disruption. Or possibly it's the fear of physical, emotional, or sexual abuse.

On the other hand, running away can be an escape for a teen overwhelmed by her own problems. These may include alcohol or drug use, failing in school, or a variety of other reasons. Talk to Tracy about what caused her to run, letting her vent feelings that you may not agree with.

Express your love and concern and your willingness to deal with whatever caused her to leave. Let her know that every problem has a solution and that you're committed as a family to finding the right one.

Problem: Rick's Bag of Pot
Yesterday when I put my son Rick's clothes away, I found a plastic bag of pot. He says it's nothing to worry about because he only smokes it occasionally—and at least he's not dropping acid like his friends. I'm horrified and worried sick. I don't want to overreact, but what should I do?

Solution: Let your son know that drug use of any kind won't be permitted under any circumstances. It is illegal. Then explore the depth of the problem.

The four levels of drug use are (1) experimentation: using drugs once or twice, just to discover what they're like; (2) recreational or social: using drugs while with friends; (3) substance abuse: using drugs to escape from reality; (4) addiction: using drugs because they control the person's life and become the top priority. To determine the level of Rick's drug use, you may need the help of a professional.

If your son is experimenting or using drugs socially, you might modify his behavior by establishing a rule and consequence, plus taking him to counseling. Random drug screenings also may be necessary to monitor his drug use. However, if he's using drugs as an escape or seems drug-dependent, intensive therapy or hospitalization might be needed.

Problem: Jackson's Unauthorized Phone Use
Jackson, twelve, spent his spring break with his grandparents who live on a fixed income. Everyone had a great time—that is until their phone bill arrived. Much to their horror,

Jackson had made three hundred dollars worth of unauthorized calls. They're willing to forget it, but I feel he should do something. He's too young to get a job. What am I to do?

Solution: Children should learn early to right a wrong whenever possible. Restitution should be part of the consequence. Therefore, provide Jackson with work at home—for example: washing windows and screens, cleaning gutters, cleaning garages and basements, doing yard work—and pay him minimum wage. He then can repay his grandparents with money he earns.

Problem: Coty Viewing a Pornographic Web Site

I recently caught my son Coty viewing a pornographic web site. I was shocked! It featured really bizarre, kinky sex. He's fourteen and says it's no big deal. How should I handle this?

Solution: Unfortunately, one of the downsides to the web is the abundance of explicit, graphic, hard-core pornographic web sites. They're easy to access and, for some kids, hard to pass up. You didn't mention where Coty's computer is located. But I always advise parents to keep computers with online access in areas like the kitchen or family room to eliminate privacy. There are simply too many sick people and too many harmful web sites. Also, many online services offer parental controls. Take advantage of them. Or invest in a program like Net Nanny or X-Detect.

Furthermore, I would talk with Coty about the damaging effects of pornography both to the viewer and to the young people portrayed.

And finally, I'd establish clear computer online guidelines, with failure to comply resulting in terminating the online service. Good rules to start with include:

1. Be very specific about the types of games, music, and so on, kids can access.
2. A parent has to be home for the child to be online.
3. The child may only visit "preapproved" chat rooms.
4. Never give personal information online.
5. Never set up meetings with people you've met online.
6. If the web site is questionable, turn the computer off.

Problem: Rori, a Pierced Eyebrow or Tattoo?

Rori is really a nice girl. She does well in school, is very compliant, and most of the time is pleasant to be around. However, recently she asked to pierce her eyebrow. If we say no to that, she wants a tattoo. Now what do we do?

Solution: I would fall back to the "You can say yes if you can say no" formula: *Is this illegal? Is this immoral? Is this going to hurt the child or someone else? Is this going to make a difference in five years? Is it inappropriate for her age?* Eyebrow piercing can be harmful. Unlike the earlobe, which is made of cartilage, the area around the eye is sensitive and loaded with little blood vessels. And tattoos can make a difference in five years because they're permanent. I would say no to both. However, there are very pretty temporary tattoos on the market that wash off with alcohol. I would offer this option.

Problem: Cooper's Gangsta Rap

My son Cooper, fifteen, is heavy into gangsta rap. Should I be concerned?

Solution: Gangsta rap is an outgrowth from hip-hop that promoted nonviolence, self-respect, and community involvement. Unfortunately, today's gangsta rap message is filled with violence, drug use, and racial hatred. Moreover, its references to aggressive sexuality and to women are demeaning and degrading.

Children are influenced by what they see and hear. For some, the impact is slight. For others, who are more vulnerable, the negative impact is considerable. Why chance it? Set a standard for your home. Establish clear guidelines concerning acceptable music. Use the Parental Advisory notices on CDs. Read the printed lyrics with your teen and discuss the messages. And finally, don't be afraid to say no.

Appendix D

■ ■ ■

HELP AT A GLANCE

Fingertip help for parenting without pressure

Through years of working with families as they cope with challenging kids, I've often heard, "I need help fast! Something at my fingertips that I can use now!" So I developed the following tips and charts for *Parenting Without Pressure* workshop participants.

Basic Parenting Principles

■ Children of all ages thrive with structure and boundaries. They need to know the rules and the consequences of breaking those rules.

■ Children also need the security of consistent, fair discipline.

■ Parents should always strive to separate children from their behavior. In other words, kids should clearly understand that although their behavior might be inappropriate or undesirable, they never are!

■ Healthy families are built through good communication that is more than hearing and understanding. Good communication involves creating a safe atmosphere that allows family members to express their thoughts and feelings.

■ Kids need positive affirmation and unconditional love to build their self-esteem.

■ Children learn more by what their parents do than by what they say. Therefore, parents should always strive to be great role models for good behavior.

Age-Appropriate Tasks

One important parenting goal is for parents to work themselves out of a job. Not only should children be required to help out around the house but also to do as much as possible for themselves.

Age 2
Put pajamas away.
Pick up toys.
Undress self.
Throw out wastepaper.
Wipe up spills.

Age 3
Comb hair.
Wash face and hands.
Dress self.
Clear place at table.
Tear lettuce for salad.
Help water plants.

Age 4
Set table.
Put groceries away.
Polish shoes with damp cloth.
Help do yard work.
Dust furniture.
Get mail.
Put dirty clothes in hamper.

Age 5
Pour own drink.
Clean mirrors and windows.
Fold clothes and put them away.
Clean out car.
Feed pet and clean its living area.
Make own sandwich.
Make bed.

Age 6
Choose clothing for day.
Shake rugs.

Water plants.
Peel vegetables.
Hang up clothes.
Tie own shoes.

Age 7
Prepare own school lunch.
Rake leaves and weeds.
Take pet for walk.
Care for own minor injuries.

Age 8
Run carpet sweeper.
Organize magazines and mail.
Take out trash.
Empty dishwasher.
Clean out silverware drawer.
Help prepare meals.
Fold and put away family laundry.

Ages 9 to 11
Wash countertops.
Keep bathroom tidy.
Help plan grocery lists.
Do dishes independently.
Wash car with supervision.
Help do laundry.
Take total care of pet.

Age 12 and Up
Do laundry independently.
Do yard work.
Prepare family meals independently.
Clean living area and own room.
If sufficiently mature, supervise young
  children.

Source: Charlene Messenger, Ph.D., Brighter Pathways, Inc., Orlando, Florida.

Suggested Age-Appropriate Boundaries

Kids, especially teens, need boundaries and supervision. The following provides a basic guideline for parents.

School Night Curfews:
Kids should be home by dinner except for preapproved special activities.

Weekend and School Holiday Curfews:

Middle school:
(with appropriate supervision)
Grade 6: 10:00 P.M.
Grades 7-8: 10:00–11:00 P.M.

High school:
Grades 9-10: 11:00–12:00 A.M.
Grades 11-12: 11:00–12:30 A.M.

Parents should always be awake or have your teen awaken you when he comes home at night.

Dating:
Middle school: Supervised group activities only
High school: Dates should be no more than two years older than your child
Suggested age for double dating: around fifteen
Suggested age for single dating: around sixteen

Other Activities:
Teenage nightclubs: These clubs are exactly like regular nightclubs except that alcohol is not served. Unfortunately, there is no age restriction and little supervision. This activity should be reserved for older teens of seventeen or eighteen.

Peer parties: Parties can be great fun. However, middle and high school students should never attend unchaperoned parties. Obtain the host parents' names, address, and phone number. Call ahead, verify the occasion, and ask questions about supervision and the alcohol policy.

Rock concerts: Older teens can attend together if they're fulfilling their responsibilities. Younger teens should never attend without adult supervision.

Going to a mall: Alright for older teens. Allow younger teens a short period of unsupervised time.

Source: Dr. John A. Crocitto

Tips for Positive Parenting

Positive parenting includes effective discipline. The following allows you to keep your head cool and your expectations clear.

Define boundaries before enforcing them. The child should know what is expected of him before he's held responsible for it. *(Parenting Without Pressure* suggests arbitration as an excellent time for this.) Remember, *if you haven't defined it, don't enforce it!*

Respond with confident decisiveness when challenged. Always respond; never react. Nothing is more destructive to parental leadership than for a parent to disintegrate during a struggle.

Distinguish between willful defiance and childish irresponsibility. Parental disciplinary response should be determined by the child's intention. Remember this when establishing consequences.

- *Willful defiance* is a deliberate act of disobedience. It occurs when the child knows what his parents expect from him and is determined to do the opposite.
- *Childish irresponsibility* results from a child's being a child. She's forgetful; she has accidents; she has a short attention span and a low frustration tolerance; and she's immature.

Reassure and teach after the confrontation is over. Children should be assured of parental love regardless of their behavior. Debriefing provides an excellent teaching opportunity. Simply ask the questions:

1. Why did you do such and such?
2. What will happen if such and such happens again?
3. How can you do it differently in the future?

Avoid impossible demands. Be absolutely sure that your child is capable of delivering what you require.

Let love be your guide! A relationship that is characterized by genuine love and affection is likely to be a healthy one, even though some parental mistakes are inevitable.

Source: Dr. James Dobson, Dare to Discipline *(Wheaton, IL: Tyndale, 1987).*

Establishing Household Rules

Establishing rules can be problematic for some parents, but made easier simply by following these guidelines.

Make sure the authority figures operate as a united front. Kids are notorious for playing divide and conquer. Privately determine your bottom line and present it as a united front. Remember, the first time they manipulate a no into a yes, you've guaranteed the behavior will be repeated.

Let the kids help. To participate in something is to have ownership in it. Therefore, allow the kids to help formulate their rules and consequences.

Be very clear about your rules and consequences. Kids are masters at finding loopholes. Therefore, be very specific about rules and consequences. For example, instead of saying, "Be home on time," say, "I expect you home at 6:00 P.M."

Explain the necessity for the rule. Rules for rules' sake won't work with today's kids. By explaining the rationale behind the rule, you've eliminated the possibility that the child will think your goal is to control every aspect of his life.

Be consistent and follow through. Consistency is the key to effective parenting. Kids need to know what to expect every single time. Therefore, make sure you follow through with rules and consequences.

Say yes to as much as you possibly can. Carefully pick your battles and say yes to as much as possible. Remember you can say yes if you can say no to these questions:
- Is this illegal?
- Is this immoral?
- Is this something that is going to hurt this child or someone else?
- Is it something that is going to make a difference in five years?
- Is it inappropriate for this child's age?

Basic Behavior Modification

Basic behavior modification is a parenting technique that rewards desired behavior and discourages undesirable behavior. To ensure long-term results, help the child identify the wonderful feeling of accomplishment and of doing things right.

Where to Start with Inappropriate Behavior

1. Specifically identify the inappropriate behavior.

2. Formulate a rule pertaining to that behavior only.

3. Attach a specific workable consequence.

4. Follow through without comment.

5. Reward good behavior!

Behavior Modification Formula:

Rule/Consequence

This is the rule. If the rule is not followed, this is the consequence.

For example: "Daily chores must be completed by 5:00. If your daily chores are not completed by 5:00, then you can't use the phone for the remainder of today."

Rule/Consequence/Incentive

To this you may add an incentive.

For example: "Daily chores must be completed by 5:00. If your daily chores are not completed by 5:00, then you can't use the phone for the remainder of today. However, if you complete your daily chores for the week, I'll add a two-dollar bonus to your allowance."

Check Your Motive

When you apply consequences, your motive should never be power, control, or revenge. Your motive simply should be to change inappropriate behavior. Therefore, present the consequence as a choice.

For example: "I don't want you to lose your phone privileges. And you don't want to lose your phone. If you lose your phone, it will be a *choice* that you make. Please complete your *daily stuff* by 5:00."

Determining Workable Consequences

Negative consequences are used to deter, change, or modify inappropriate behavior. Consequences should never include corporal punishment and should never strip a child of his dignity or damage his self-esteem.

When Determining Consequences:

1. Remember that less is better.

2. Keep the consequence short term.

3. Make sure the consequence fits the transgression.

When Possible, Consequences Should Include:

1. The loss of something the child values

2. A teaching component

3. Restitution

The Different Types of Consequences:

Natural consequences: Take place with no parental intervention

Logical consequences: Require intervention and are related

Leverage points: Are those things a child values and holds dear. The best consequences are those that are logical and use a child's leverage points.

When parents determine consequences, it's important to remember what they owe their children:

1. A roof over their heads

2. Clothing

3. Three meals a day

4. A great deal of unconditional love

Everything else can be used as a consequence.

However, one word of caution: Don't use constructive activities such as Boy Scouts or soccer as consequences. When you pull positive things from a child's life, a vacuum is created that is often filled with something else.

Everyday Things That Can Be Used as Consequences:

■ Loss of phone, car, or TV privileges

■ Loss of allowance or lunch money

■ Extra household chores or yard work

■ Assigned written essays

■ Grounding to room, the house, or the house and yard

■ No use of favorite items such as bicycles, skateboards, or video games

The Magic of Incentives

Positive consequences or incentives are intrinsic and extrinsic rewards that reinforce good behavior and/or motivate the child.

Intrinsic rewards:
Praise
Appreciation
Encouragement
Acknowledgment

Extrinsic rewards:
Special privileges
Money
Material items
Tokens

For Younger Children

Activities and Privileges

Later bedtime
Trip to toy store
Special game with Mom and Dad
Extra story
Trip to a fast-food restaurant

Bowling with friends
Sleep over with friends
Bike ride with Mom and Dad
Stickers and appreciation notes

For Teenagers

Material Items, Activities, and Privileges

Clothes	Driver's license	Later bedtime
Trip to beach/lake	Use of family car	Gas money
Dating privileges	Shoes	Tokens for video-games
Radio	Skating	Nintendo
Haircuts/perms	Additional allowance	Sleep in on weekends
Private phone	Room decorating	TV in room
Stereo	Hobby materials	Computer time to chat
Practice driving time	Part-time job	with friends or play
Extended curfew	Sports equipment	games
Tapes/CDs	Movie rental	

When to Use Incentives:

1. To reward very good behavior
2. To reinforce a child struggling with a particular behavior
3. When nothing else is working

Setting Up Token Economies:

Rewarding with tokens that can be cashed in for rewards is a great way to apply incentives. Poker chips make excellent tokens. However, if you have more than one child, make sure they have different color chips. Likewise, when you use tokens, be very specific about the value of each token. Finally, never use extrinsic rewards without also using intrinsic rewards.

Tips for Younger Children

When Dealing with Inappropriate Behavior

Because younger children have shorter attention spans, deal with inappropriate behavior immediately. Lee Canter, in his excellent book *Assertive Discipline for Parents*, offers these suggestions.

Broken Record

1. Request to change behavior
2. A repeated request to change
3. The offer of a choice
4. Follow through on the choice

For example: (1) "Please stop running in the house." (2) "Please stop running in the house." (3) "Either stop running in the house or go outside until dinner." (4) "Okay, please go outside until dinner."

Do What I Want First

A child must complete what the parent wants before doing what she wants. ***For example:*** "Please pick-up your toys and then you can go outside to play."

Making Rules for Young Children

1. Look at the child, ideally on an eye-to-eye level.
2. Appropriately touch the child on the arm or shoulder.
3. Establish the necessity for the rule.
4. Formulate the rule and attach a consequence.
5. Ask him to repeat the rule and consequence to you.
6. Write it down.

For example: "When you leave your bike outside at night, it's likely to be either hit by a car or stolen. Therefore, we need a rule. And the rule is this: If you don't put your bike in the garage when you come in for dinner, you'll not be able to ride it the next day. Now, repeat the rule back to me. 'If I don't put my bike in the garage when I come in for dinner, I will not be able to ride it the next day.' That's right. Now let's write it in the book."

Source: Lee Canter, Assertive Discipline for Parents *(New York, NY: Harper & Row, 1985).*

More Tips for Younger Children

Again, because younger children have shorter attention spans, deal with inappropriate behavior immediately. Dr. Thomas Phelan, in his excellent book *1-2-3 Magic: Effective Discipline for Children 2-12*, offers these suggestions.

1-2-3 Magic

When a change in behavior doesn't occur after you make a request, this is what you do:

1. You look down at the child and hold up your index finger and say, "That's one." That is all you're allowed to say.
2. After a few seconds, if no change in the behavior occurs, you say, "That's two."
3. After a few seconds, if still no change in the behavior occurs, you simply say, "That's three. Now take a five-minute time-out."

Three counts within a fifteen- to twenty-minute period earn a time-out. To successfully implement this technique, you say absolutely nothing else. By continuing to talk, you take the responsibility for the child's behavior.

For example: When Larry was teasing his little brother, Mom asked him to stop. However, he continued. She simply held up her index finger and said, "That's one." A few minutes later he started teasing his brother again. Mom responded with "That's two." Unfortunately, after a few minutes Larry again started in on his brother. Mom handled the situation by saying, "That's three. Now take a five-minute time-out."

Tell your child what to do instead of what not to do. We have a tendency to visualize what we hear. Therefore, verbalize the behavior you want from the child, not the behavior you don't want. For example, instead of saying, "Stop hitting your brother!" say, "Play nicely with your brother."

Source: Thomas Phelan, Ph.D., 1-2-3 Magic: Effective Discipline for Children 2-12
(Glen Ellyn, IL: Child Management, Inc., 1995).

Diffuse an Escalating Situation

As parents, we have all experienced the horror of making a request of a child only to have him respond with "I'm not going to do it!" We usually then respond with anger and frustration, "Yes you are!" Only to have the kid scream, "No I'm not!" And you now yell, "Yes you are!" And on and on it goes until everyone is completely out of control, the kid has been grounded for six years, and he still isn't doing what you asked. The following techniques can diffuse the escalating situation and get the family back on track.

1. *Acknowledge the child's feelings.* It's not necessary to *agree* with the feeling to acknowledge it. You simply are putting a name to the feeling, such as angry, frustrated, annoyed, discouraged, sad, hurt, uncomfortable, or disappointed.

2. *Provide a choice or alternative.* Here you simply offer another option.

3. *Disengage from the behavior.* It takes at least *two* people to fight. Don't argue about anything at any time other than arbitration.

Sample dialogue: Respond to escalating behavior with "I can see how frustrated and angry you are and I'm sorry. I know things are bad for you right now, but I promise they're going to be better. Let's find a solution for this at arbitration."

Sample dialogue: Respond to noncompliant behavior with "I can see how frustrated and angry you are and I'm sorry. But whether you choose to do this or not will be a choice that you make." If the child chooses not to comply, the disobeying clause/rule would apply.

Sample dialogue: Respond to noncompliant behavior by offering a choice. "Sam, you need to turn the TV off. Sam, you have a choice to either turn the TV off or lose the use of the car tomorrow. I'm going to count to three, and if you haven't turned off the TV, then I'll know what your choice is."

Tips for ADD/ADHD Kids

PWOP works exceptionally well with ADD or ADHD children. Because of PWOP's concrete format, everyone knows what to expect every time. Additionally, the following tips will make your parenting easier and more effective.

Learn everything about ADD/ADHD, its associated difficulties, and its impact on the family. ADD/ADHD children are not like other children. Consequently, many parents become very frustrated when parenting techniques that worked before will not work as well with these children. It's important for parents to have a clear understanding of ADD/ADHD and its associated difficulties and to be realistic with parental expectations.

Take very good care of yourself and your marriage. Parenting an ADHD child is a challenge, and parents often feel overwhelmed. However, parents can avoid emotional overload by effectively managing their time. Because ADHD children require a great deal of time, plan your schedules accordingly. Parents should take time for themselves by developing their own interest, strengths, and goals. If married, they also should focus on the relationship apart from the kids. Also important for parents is to take time to join an ADD/ADHD support group that can provide plenty of information, guidance, and support.

Develop a behavior management program (such as PWOP) that allows you to be concrete, concise, and consistent with discipline. *Parenting Without Pressure* furnishes an objective, nonmanipulative parenting tool that enables parents to be firm, fair, consistent, and positive with discipline. It also provides a format to teach accountability, responsibility, and consequences for behavior and allows for easy assessment in determining what is working, what is not working, and where to go from here.

Provide structure. Create a structured environment by establishing order, organization, and predictability. ADHD children do best when they know what to expect every time. This structure includes establishing routines, simplifying specific tasks, and organizing your child's time by setting schedules.

Use supervision and intervention. Because ADHD children are highly impulsive, they require a great deal of supervision. Additionally, because ADHD children often have difficulty learning from past mistakes, parents should shift their focus to an intervening action. Parents then can intervene with behavior before it's a problem and be quicker at praise than criticism. It also enables parents to reinforce good habits with praise and rewards.

Be assertive with communication. Assertive communication involves being very clear, direct, and reasonable. It simply communicates, "I say what I mean and mean what I say every single time."

Do whatever possible to enhance self-esteem. ADHD children often suffer from poor self-esteem. Parents can help by utilizing PWOP to deal with inappropriate behavior while shifting focus to what the kids are doing right. Also, parents can help by developing the habit of praising children at least four times daily. Additionally, because ADHD children are impulsive, aggressive, and bossy, they often have little positive social contact that provides the basis for a healthy self-esteem. Parents can help by encouraging areas where children are good. Furthermore, when social interaction takes place, carefully plan ahead and monitor the situation.

Source: Charlene Messenger, Ph.D., Brighter Pathways, Inc., Orlando, Florida.

Tips for Noncompliant Kids

Noncompliant kids break rules and refuse to follow through with the consequences, refuse to comply when specific requests are made, and run away from home. Parenting noncompliant kids requires the patience of a saint, the endurance of a long-distance runner, and the courage of a bullfighter. However, it's not an impossible task if parents remember the following.

Provide something to lose. Noncompliant kids feel they have nothing to lose. And when children feel they have nothing to lose, they have no reason to cooperate. This feeling often results when a parent has taken everything as a consequence and the child simply has shut down. Also, it occurs when parents have little or no control and the child does as he pleases. Instead of this lose/lose situation, make it a win/win situation. Parents can accomplish this by identifying an incentive (something the child really wants that the parent can control, such as the use of an automobile or a private phone line), then allowing the child daily to buy the privilege with his compliant behavior. This means if he breaks a rule, he'll take the consequence, he'll comply if you make a request, and he doesn't run away but hangs in there when the going gets tough.

Offer parental approval. As tough as they seem, these kids still long for parental approval. Unfortunately, they often perceive parental frustration and anger as rejection, which adds to the "You don't care, so why should I" feeling. As parents, work diligently on the issue of compliance, and dismantle the hostility by creating an atmosphere for cooperation. By using the cause-effect-incentive approach, you can correct negative behavior while shifting your focus to what the child is doing right.

Eliminate power struggles, which only add to a child's feelings of rejection. When a parent finds himself embroiled in a power struggle with a teen, he generally will lose. Unfortunately, some parents develop a "them versus us" attitude. They erroneously think that withdrawal of parental love and affection will snap the kids in line. Just the opposite happens. Kids are left with feelings of rejection that add to "You don't care, so why should I?" Parental goals should include teaching responsibility and decision making, not obedience by control. Give up the struggle without giving up the authority, and communicate to your child that there is no "them versus us" in this household. You're on the same side.

Enhance poor self-esteem. Often noncompliant children have bottomed out with their self-esteem. The only success they know is successful failure. Consequently, they'll go to any length to be accepted by their peers. It's vitally important, therefore, that parents help enhance these kids' self-esteems. You can accomplish this by making your child feel wanted, cared for, and accepted at home. Daily find something to do together that you both enjoy. Ask her opinion or advice about something, and listen. And finally, remind him of what he's doing right rather than focusing on the inappropriate behavior.

Screen for substance abuse. Many noncompliant children have not learned appropriate problem-solving or coping skills. Therefore, they tend to mask their feelings with alcohol and drugs. Because alcohol and drugs will have a negative effect on every aspect of a child's life, parents must deal with this first. Seek treatment immediately.

Tips for Good Communication

Always treat children with courtesy, respect, and understanding. Good communication flows from mutual respect and understanding among family members. When children are treated with the same courtesy and understanding that parents give their best friends, it sends a strong message of love and support. Be generous with comments like please and thank you. Make requests instead of giving orders. And always be quick to say, "I'm sorry," when you're wrong.

Listen actively by repeating your child's feelings with empathy and understanding. Simple acknowledgment of the child's feelings will always get you a lot of mileage. Not only do you validate the child, but also you put her in a position to then hear what you have to say. Remember, you don't have to agree with a child's feelings in order to describe what she's feeling. You simply put yourself in your child's shoes and don't judge, offer advice, or ask a lot of questions.

Cool off before you talk, and choose your words carefully. Children really do believe what a parent tells them, and they'll always reach up or stoop down to parental expectations. Therefore, make sure that what you say is positive and builds up rather than tears down.

Make sure your nonverbal communication is positive. Dr. Albert Mehrabian states in his book *Silent Messages* that 55 percent of communication is nonverbal body language. Thirty-eight percent is tone of voice. Only 7 percent is content. Check your body language and the tone of your voice. Make sure both are positive.

Remember, if you want to be heard, you first must be available and listen. Take the time to make yourself available. Only when a child genuinely feels he has been heard and understood does a parent have a prayer that the child will listen. Create an atmosphere where it is safe for kids to explore their thoughts and feelings even if you don't agree.

Hold weekly family meetings. Weekly family meetings provide all family members with a platform to be heard and understood. They also create a format for families to formulate rules, determine operating boundaries, and deal with problem areas while those areas are still minor.

Coping with Stress

Recognize signs of distress. They include giving up and becoming depressed; experiencing an inability to concentrate; becoming argumentative, irritable, anxious; or developing stress-related illnesses, such as heart palpitations, insomnia, headaches, high blood pressure, neck and back pain, ulcers, and stomachaches.

Eliminate the threat of stress. Don't be afraid of it. Instead, put yourself in control by finding appropriate ways to manage your stress. These techniques are very individual and will vary from person to person.

Lower your expectations of yourself and others. Becoming more realistic with your expectations can be both freeing and empowering.

Be optimistic. Remember that people who say, "I can," and people who say, "I can't," are both right. Look at new challenges as chances to grow and learn.

Work off tension through physical exercise. Chemicals released during exercise produce a mood-elevating effect. Try jogging, swimming, gardening, working out, or walking.

Take short breaks—balance work and play. Schedule time for work and recreational activities. A short break might include a good stretch or a fifteen-minute nap. Both can work wonders. A walk at lunchtime will give you more energy and will reduce stress.

Get away from it all. Go to the movies, watch TV, read a book, or visit a friend. Plan a camping trip or other mini-vacation. Sometimes a change of scenery can give you a new perspective on life and reduce stress. Take time for hobbies; they can become a refuge in a storm.

Get adequate sleep and eat a healthy diet during times of stress. Stress causes blood sugar to fluctuate wildly, causing mood swings, irritability, fatigue, and food cravings. Eat lightly and more often and include complex carbohydrates for energy. Avoid fats and sugars, and drink plenty of water. Also, cut back on stimulants such as caffeine and nicotine.

Avoid self-medication. Alcohol and tranquilizers are depressants that will depress you and add to your stress.

Get professional help. If tension and stress are long term and continuous, don't be afraid to get professional help.

Source: Dr. Penny Lukin

Making Home a Positive Place

Families share more than space. They're committed to one another, they spend time together, and they share values, warm memories, and family traditions. This isn't a dry run for a better show at a later date. This is the only family your children will ever know. You owe it to them and yourself to make it great!

Celebrate the uniqueness of all family members. Appreciate the individuality of each family member. Remember, kids don't have to be clones of Mom and Dad to be acceptable. How different can a parent allow a child to be? Ask yourself: *"Is this illegal?" "Is it immoral?" "Is it something that is going to make a difference in five years?" "Is it going to hurt the child or someone else?" "Is it inappropriate for the child's age?"* If you can say no to these questions, you can say yes to the child's uniqueness.

Create a safe environment. Make your home a safe place for all family members. In addition to not permitting physical confrontations, don't allow verbal mistreatment. Insist that all family members treat one another with courtesy, kindness, and respect.

Grab every opportunity to spend unstructured time. It takes time to get to know a young person, to feel her hurts, and to understand her problems. Look for opportunities to spend time with your children. For example, play catch or shoot baskets, play video games or board games, build a snowman or sandcastle, help with homework or daily chores, go for a walk, ride bikes, or simply read a story.

Plan family fun. Spending time together provides happy memories that the family can draw on during difficult times. These might include summer picnics, trips to the beach or mountains, backyard barbecues, or even learning a sport together as a family. Use arbitration as an opportunity to discuss and plan a monthly family time. Then make it a priority and put it on the calendar.

Teach values. Families teach children societal rules and behavioral expectations. Additionally, children learn morals, values, and attitudes from the family. They also learn about relationships and what is considered important. By your actions and your words, teach about love, honesty, courage, self-discipline, chastity, loyalty, fairness, empathy, tolerance, respect, and right from wrong.

Establish family traditions. Another way to make memories and have fun is through family traditions. Traditions simply celebrate the family, cultivate family identity, build hopefulness, and cement family ties. They don't have to be elaborate affairs, just relevant to your family. Your family rituals or traditions might be the special way you celebrate the holidays, acknowledge a family member's milestone (such as a birthday), or honor a family member's achievement (such as a good report card).

NOTES

CHAPTER ONE: HOME SWEET BATTLEGROUND

1. Beth Winship, "Traits Teens Should Learn on Their Way to Maturity," *The Orlando Sentinel,* January 1, 1987, E6. Used with permission.

CHAPTER TWO: YOUR KIDS AND THE REAL WORLD

1. William R. Brown, "Relationships Between Abuse of Alcohol/Drugs and Juvenile Offenders," Report for Metropolitan Alcoholism Council of Central Florida, Orlando, FL, March 1987, 40.
2. Debbie Cenziper, "Squeezing In Family Time," *The Orlando Sentinel,* August 8, 1994, D4.
3. Ken Bryson and Lynee Casper, *Household and Family Characteristics: March 1997,* P20-509, Bureau of Census, April 1998; Bureau of Census, "Able F-&. Types of Family—Families (All Races) by Median and Mean Income; 1947 to 1996," www.census.gov/hhes/income/histinc/f07.htm.
4. As quoted by Robert Wallace, "Responsibility Paves Way to Freedom," *The Orlando Sentinel,* September 18, 1990, Style Section.
5. U.S. Department of Labor, Employment Characteristics of Families in 1997, 1998.
6. Rudolf Dreikurs, M.D., *Coping with Children's Misbehavior, A Parent's Guide* (New York: Hawthorn, 1972).

CHAPTER THREE: RULES WE CAN LIVE BY

1. Laura Shapiro, "The Myth of Quality Time," *Newsweek,* May 12, 1997, 64.
2. Quoted material through the end of the chapter is taken from Dr. James Dobson, *The Strong-Willed Child* (Wheaton, IL: Tyndale, 1987), 29-33. Used by permission.

CHAPTER FOUR: WHAT THEY DO IS WHAT THEY GET

1. Dr. Becky Baily, *There's Gotta Be a Better Way* (Orlando, FL: Learning In Action, 1994), 270.
2. Rudolf Dreikurs, M.D., *Children: The Challenge* (New York: Plume, 1990), 76-81.
3. From Colleen Alexander-Roberts, *ADHD & Teens: A Parent's Guide to Making It Through the Tough Years* (Dallas, TX: Taylor Publishing, 1995), 4.
4. Howard Chua-Eoan, "Special Report: Troubled Kids Escaping from the Darkness," *Time,* May 31, 1999, 64.
5. Alexander-Roberts, 92.
6. S. E. Dubuque, "A Parent's Survival Guide to Childhood Depression." King of Prussia, PA: The Center for Applied Psychology, Inc., 1996, http://www.nmhaorg/children/green/chdeplst.cfm.

7. From James Garbarino, Ph.D., *Lost Boys: Why Our Sons Turn Violent and How We Can Save Them* (New York: The Free Press, 1999), 50.

8. From Garbarino, 71.

9. Garbarino, 167.

10. Lillian Katz, "How Can We Strengthen Children's Self-Esteem?" Eric Clearinghouse on Elementary and Early Children Education, University of Illinois, http://ericeece.org/.

11. Dr. Laura Schlessinger, *How Could You Do That?* (New York: Harper Collins, 1996), 89.

CHAPTER FIVE: TALKING DOWN A STORM

1. "Family Meals: On the Verge of Extinction," *Parents of Teenagers*, February/March 1991, 27.

2. As quoted by Cheri Fuller, *365 Ways to Develop Your Child's Values* (Colorado Springs, CO: Piñon Press, 1994), no. 262.

3. Nancy Samalin, "Problem: Disagreeing in Front of Kids," *Bottom Line Personal*, July 1, 1996, 1.

4. Darryl Owens, "Family Meetings: Talk with a Purpose," *The Orlando Sentinel*, August 17, 1994, E1, 3.

5. Lee and Marlene Canter, *Assertive Discipline for Parents* (New York: Harper & Row, 1985), 19. Used by permission.

6. Canter, 19.

7. Thomas Phelan, Ph.D., *1-2-3 Magic: Effective Discipline for Children 2-12* (Glen Ellyn, IL: Child Management, Inc., 1995), 20-21. Used by permission.

8. Thomas Gordon, as quoted by Don Dinkmeyer and Gary D. McKay in *The Parent's Guide for STEP* (Systematic Training for Effective Parenting of Teens) (Circle Pines, MN: American Guidance Service, 1983), 103.

9. Shannon Brownlee, "Inside the Teen Brain," *U.S. News and World Report*, August 9, 1999.

10. Brownlee, 47.

CHAPTER SIX: TOTS AND TEENS

1. From Jay Kesler, ed., with Ronald Beers, *Parents and Teenagers* (Wheaton, IL: Victor, 1984), 181.

2. Joe Klein, "The Predator Problem," *Newsweek*, April 29, 1996, 32.

3. James E. Gardner, *Understanding, Helping, Surviving the Turbulent Teens* (San Diego, CA: Oak Tree Publications, 1982), 198.

4. Dr. Kevin Leman, *Smart Kids, Stupid Choices* (Ventura, CA: Regal, 1987), 110.

5. "Teen Pregnancies: High Rates, Higher Cost," *US News & World Report*, April 15, 1996, 16.

6. Kathleen McCoy and Charles Wibbelsman, M.D., *Crisis Proof Your Teenager* (New York: Bantam, 1991), 124.

7. Dan Korem, *Streetwise Parents, Foolproof Kids* (Colorado Springs, CO: NavPress, 1992), 171.

8. "Holiday Dieting," *Parents/Teenagers*, November/December 1992.

9. Ann Gerbart, "Teens Search for Perfection: Cosmetic procedures: More young women seek quick fix," *The Orlando Sentinel*, August 31, 1999, E5.

10. Ross Campbell, M.D., *How to Really Love Your Teenager* (Wheaton, IL: Victor, 1985), 25.

11. From Jay Kesler, ed., with Ronald Beers, *Parents and Teenagers* (Wheaton, IL: Victor, 1984), 180.

12. Kesler, 180.

13. Kesler, 180.

14. Kesler, 180.

15. Colleen Alexander-Roberts, *ADHD & Teens: A Parent's Guide to Making It Through the Tough Years* (Dallas, TX: Taylor Publishing, 1995), 85.

16. Linda and Richard Eyre, *Teaching Your Children Values* (New York: Simon & Schuster, 1993), 159.

17. Eyre, 221.

18. Kesler, 180.

19. Dr. Debora Phillips with Fred Bernstein, *How to Give Your Child a Great Self-Image* (New York: The Penguin Group, 1991), 50-51.

20. Dr. Peter Favaro, *Smart Parenting* (Chicago: Contemporary Books, 1995), 19.

21. Dr. James Dobson, *Home with a Heart* (Wheaton, IL: Tyndale, 1996), 4-5. Used by permission.

22. Dr. Pat Palmer with Melissa Froehner, *Teen Esteem* (San Luis Obispo, CA: Impact Publishers, 1995), 23.

23. Kesler, 181.

24. Fritz Ridenour, *What Teenagers Wish Their Parents Knew About Kids* (Waco, TX: Word, 1982), 48.

25. Barbara Gregg, "100 Ways for Parents to Show Appreciation," *Seminole Outlook,* January 5, 1989. Used by permission.

26. Ridenour, 48.

CHAPTER SEVEN: SAVED BY THE BELL

1. "How Parents and Families Can Help Their Children Do Better in School," U.S. Department of Education, http://www.kidsource.com/kidsource/content/better-school.html.

2. http://www.kidsource.com/kidsource/content/betterschool.html.

3. "High School Students with a Job," *Bottom Line,* March 30, 1993.

4. Susan Barbieri, "Dropout: A Matter of Self-Esteem," *The Orlando Sentinel,* March 30, 1990, E14.

5. Kathryn Black, "What to Do About Bullies," *McCall's,* October 1996, 130.

CHAPTER EIGHT: HOW CAN I LOVE YOU?

1. Patricia Jakubowski and A. J. Lane, *Assertive Option* (Champaign, IL: Research Press, 1978), 80-81. Used by permission.

2. Laurie Tarkan, "Relax: Stress Relief Is a Few Techniques Away," *The Orlando Sentinel*, July 19, 1994, E4.

3. Pam Smith, *Eat Well, Live Well* (Lake Mark, FL: Creation House, 1992), 55.

4. Mary G. Durkin, *Making Your Family Work* (Chicago: Thomas More Press, 1988), 55.

5. Christian Hageseth, as quoted by Ellen Javernick in "He Who Laughs Last," *Parents Magazine*, September 1989, 6.

6. Dave and Claudia Arp, *52 Dates for You and Your Mate* (Nashville, TN: Thomas Nelson, 1993).

CHAPTER NINE: LOVING UNCONDITIONALLY

1. Ross Campbell, *How to Really Love Your Teenager* (Wheaton, IL: Victor, 1985), 45.
2. Campbell, 48.
3. Maurice Wagner, *The Sensation of Being Somebody* (Grand Rapids MI: Zondervan, 1975), 34.
4. Greg Wallace, "Gang Member Speaks Out on Esteem," *The Orlando Sentinel*, E4.
5. Wagner, 34.
6. Wallace, E4.
7. Wagner, 36.
8. William Glasser, as quoted by Stephanie Marston in *The Magic of Encouragement* (New York: Pocket Books, 1990), 215.
9. Jerry Adler, "Kids Growing Up Scared," *Newsweek*, January 10, 1994, 44.
10. Darryl Owens, "Successful Stepfamilies," *The Orlando Sentinel*, March 31, 1995, E6.
11. "The Rise of the Stepfamily: How parents and kids mix and match and make new families work," *U.S. News and World Report*, November 29, 1999, 59.
12. "American Agenda: Growing Up Without Fathers," *World News Tonight with Peter Jennings*, American Online, December 13, 1994.
13. "Missing Dads: One Out of Three Teens Have Lost Contact," *Parents/Teenagers*, November/December 1992.
14. Sandra Mathers, "Grandparents Learn to Be Parents—Again," *The Orlando Sentinel*, October 25, 1995, D3.
15. Laura Shapiro, "The Myth of Quality Time," *Newsweek*, May 12, 1997, 65.
16. "Just a Routine School Shooting," *Time*, May 31, 1999.
17. Joseph P. Shapiro with Missy Daniel, "Teenage Wasteland? The passage from age 10 to 14 is very tricky, but it need not be the pits," *U.S. News & World Report*, October 23, 1997, 87.
18. Kathleen McCoy and Charles Wibbelsman, *Crisis Proof Your Teenager* (New York: Bantam, 1991), 62.
19. Jennifer Allen, "The Incredible Healing Power of Family Rituals," *McCall's*, February 1993, 73.
20. Paul and Leisa Tigpen, *52 Simple Ways to Build Family Traditions* (Nashville, TN: Thomas Nelson), 18.
21. Margaret Newman, *Stepfamily Realities: How to Overcome Difficulties and Have a Happy Family* (Oakland, CA: New Harbinger Publications, 1994), 4-5. Used by permission.
22. Lawrence Kutner, "The Rules Are Yours but the Children Aren't," *The Orlando Sentinel*, February 17, 1994, E3.
23. James Garbarino, Ph.D., *Raising Children in a Socially Toxic Environment* (San Francisco, CA: Jossey-Bass Publication, 1995).

BIBLIOGRAPHY

Alexander-Roberts, Colleen. *ADHD & Teens: A Parent's Guide to Making It Through the Tough Years*. Dallas TX: Taylor Publishing, 1995.

Campbell, Ross. *How to Really Love Your Teenager*. Wheaton, IL: Victor, 1985.

Canter, Lee and Marlene. *Assertive Discipline for Parents*. New York: Harper & Row, 1985.

Cline, Foster, M.D., and Jim Fay. *Parenting with Love and Logic*. Colorado Springs, CO: Piñon Press, 1992.

Colen, Robert, and Geoffrey Stokes. *Sex and the American Teenager*. New York: Harper & Row, 1985.

Dendy, Chris A. Zeigler. *Teenagers with ADD: A Parent's Guide*. Bethesda, MD: Woodbine House, 1995.

Dinkmeyer, Don, and Gary D. McKay. *The Parent's Guide for STEP* (Systematic Training for Effective Parenting of Teens). Circle Pines, MN: American Guidance Service, 1983.

Dobson, James. *Dare to Discipline*. Wheaton, IL: Tyndale, 1987.

Dobson, James. *Home with a Heart*. Wheaton, IL: Tyndale, 1996.

Dobson, James. *The Strong-Willed Child*. Wheaton, IL: Tyndale, 1987.

Dreikurs, Rudolf, M.D. *Children: The Challenge*. New York: Plume, 1990.

Durkin, Mary G. *Making Your Family Work*. Chicago: Thomas More Press, 1988.

Einstein, Elizabeth, and Linda Albert. *Strengthening Your Stepfamily*. Circle Pines, MN: American Guidance Service, 1986.

Elkind, David. *The Hurried Child*. Reading, MA: Addison-Wesley Publishing, 1988.

Eyre, Linda and Richard. *Teaching Your Children Responsibility*. New York: Simon & Schuster, 1984.

Eyre, Linda and Richard. *Teaching Your Children Values*. New York: Simon & Schuster, 1993.

Faber, Adele, and Elaine Mazlish. *Liberated Parents—Liberated Children*. New York: Avon Books, 1975.

Faber, Adele, and Elaine Mazlish. *How to Talk So Kids Will Listen and Listen So Kids Will Talk*. New York: Avon Books, 1982.

Favaro, Peter. *Smart Parenting: An Easy Approach to Raising Happy, Well-Adjusted Kids*. Chicago: Contemporary Books, 1994.

Garbarino, James E., Ph.D. *Raising Children in a Socially Toxic Environment*. San Francisco, CA: Jossey-Bass Publication, 1995.

Garbarino, James E., Ph.D. *Lost Boys: Why Our Sons Turn Violent and How We Can Save Them*. New York: The Free Press, 1999.

Gardner, James E., Ph.D. *Understanding, Helping, Surviving the Turbulent Teens*. San Diego, CA: Oak Tree Publications, 1982.

Giannetti, Charlene, and Margaret Sagarese. *Parenting 911*. New York: Broadway Books, 1999.

Glenn, Stephen H., and Jane Nelsen, Ed.D. *Raising Self-Reliant Children in a Self-Indulgent World.* Rocklin, CA: Prima Publishing & Communication, 1989.

Jaksa, Peter. *25 Stupid Mistakes Parents Make.* Los Angeles: Lowell House, 1998.

Jakubowski, Patricia, and A. J. Lane. *The Assertive Option.* Champaign, IL: Research Press, 1975.

Kesler, Jay, ed., with Ronald Beers. *Parents and Teenagers.* Wheaton, IL: Victor, 1984.

Kolodny, Robert C. and Nancy; Thomas Bratter; and Cheryl Deep. *How to Survive Your Adolescent's Adolescence.* Boston: Little, Brown, 1984.

Kruger, Caryl Waller. *Working Parent, Happy Child.* Nashville, TN: Abingdon, 1990.

Leman, Kevin. *Smart Kids, Stupid Choices.* Ventura, CA: Regal, 1987.

MacKenzie, Robert. *Setting Limits.* Rocklin, CA: Prima Publishing. 1998.

Magid, Ken, M.D., and Carole A. McKelvery. *High Risk: Children Without a Conscience.* New York: Bantam, 1988.

Messenger, Charlene, Ph.D. *Secret of the Third Little Pig.* Orlando, FL: Brighter Pathway, Inc. 1999.

Nelsen, Jane; Carol Erwin; and Carol Delzer. *Positive Discipline for Single Parents.* Rocklin, CA: Prima Publishing, 1994.

Nelsen, Jane, and Lynn Lott. *Positive Discipline for Teenagers.* Rocklin,CA: Prima Publishing, 1994.

Newman, Margaret. *Stepfamily Realities: How to Overcome Difficulties and Have a Happy Family.* Oakland, CA: New Harbinger Publications, 1994.

Phelan, Thomas, Ph.D. *1-2-3 Magic: Effective Discipline for Children 2-12.* Glen Ellyn, IL: Child Management, Inc., 1995.

Phelan, Thomas, Ph.D. *Surviving Your Adolescents: How to Manage and Let Go of Your 13-18 Year Olds.* Glen Ellyn, IL: Child Management, Inc., 1998.

Phillips, Debora, and Fred Bernstein. *How to Give Your Child a Great Self-Image.* New York: Penguin, 1989.

Pollack, William. *Real Boys: Rescuing Our Sons from the Myths of Boyhood.* New York: Henry Holt, 1998.

Ridenour, Fritz. *What Teenagers Wish Their Parents Knew About Kids.* Waco, TX: Word, 1982.

Shimberg, Elaine Fantle. *Blending Families.* New York: Berkley Publishing Group, 1999.

Weinhaus, Evonne, and Karen Friedman. *Stop Struggling with Your Teen.* New York: Penguin, 1988.

Wesson, Carolyn McLenahan. *Teen Troubles: How to Keep Them from Becoming Tragedies.* New York: Walker and Co., 1988.

Wyckoff, Jerry, and Barbara Unell. *How to Discipline Your Six- to Twelve- Year Old . . . Without Losing Your Mind.* New York: Doubleday, 1991.

ABOUT THE AUTHOR

When her first husband died in the Vietnam War, Teresa Langston was catapulted into circumstances that were quite different from the ideal life she had planned. Suddenly, she was a grieving and devastated widow and a single mother of an eighteen-month-old daughter. She subsequently married a man with three children, and soon had another daughter. As she experienced firsthand the challenges of parenthood, she began a journey that led to the *Parenting Without Pressure* philosophy.

A graduate of the University of Central Florida, Teresa Langston is recognized nationally for her expertise in the parenting field. A writer, speaker, and workshop leader since 1987, she resides in Longwood, Florida, with her husband, Herbert.

INDEX